Mary, Mary Quite Contrary

Fourth Edition
Or
[1]Does the Lord Jesus Christ Want women
To Rule as Elders in His Church ?

By David Clarke

This is not confidential and is for all to read.
Grace be with all them that love our Lord Jesus Christ in sincerity.

2

First Published: 16th January 2003
Abshott Publications
11 Hayling Close
Fareham
Hampshire
PO 14 3AE

E-mail: nbpttc@yahoo.co.uk

www.BiertonParticularBaptists.co.uk

ISBN 978-1-4717-4461-7

1 FOREWORD BY DR. KEN MATTO

We live in a day of rank apostasy. That apostasy is not limited to the unbelieving world because much of it is accepted by the Christian world. David Clarke hits head on one of the tenets of the apostasy which has exploded internationally. A time like this had been prophesied by Isaiah. Isaiah 3:12 (KJV) As for my people, children are their oppressors, and women rule over them. O my people, they which lead thee cause thee to err, and destroy the way of thy paths. The tenet which David Clarke hits head on is the one of women preachers and women elders in the churches. Isaiah states that women were ruling over the people of God, when the men should have been in leadership roles. The Scripture states that "they which lead thee cause thee to err." In this book you will find a confrontation between elders and the word of God. When church leaders neglect the truths of Scripture and base everything they believe on as their "personal opinion", then the paths have been destroyed for the Christian, as Isaiah teaches.

One of the outgrowths of the charismatic movement, is the teaching that women are just as qualified as men to be elders and pastors. This is not to say that women are lacking leadership qualities but the Bible is very clear that they are not to rule over men and are not to have rule in the churches. It is unfortunate that many feminized men in the church kowtow behind the concept that disallowing women rule in the churches is not showing them love. The reality is that being disobedient to the commands of Scripture is nothing more than rebellion against God. 1 Samuel 15:3 speaks about rebellion being as the sin of witchcraft. God has given specific instructions concerning the churches and their structure and who are we to claim that we know more than God.

The deep apostasy which many churches have accepted is made visible in this book but not only churches, Bible colleges have also acquiesced to disobeying the Bible and have endorsed women rulers in the church. It is a shame that those who bring the truth are considered the troublemakers in the churches. Tell me, what kind of love do you show someone when you actually help them to be disobedient to God? Will they still love you when they are in hell paying for their sins of rebellion? It is time for Christian men to step up and be men. 1 Corinthians 16:13 (KJV) Watch ye, stand fast in the faith, quit you like men, be strong. This book needs to be in the library of all Christians to help them oppose the incursion of women rulers in the church. It is still not too late to bring about a repentance on the part of church leaders for allowing themselves to be swayed by false teaching. A strong church obeys God, a weak and dying one disobeys God, regardless of how many attend.

Dr. Ken Matto

Scion of Zion Internet Ministry

www.scionofzion.com

British Church Newspaper (Book Review)

One of the most profound changes that has come over our society in the last century is married women going out to work.

This trend was given a considerable boost by the need to recruit female workers in the factories during WW2.

Many other factors have contributed since then. They range from labour saving devices in the home to the unpredictable nature of modem marriage.

Things have now progressed to the point where women are taking over the professions including the ordained ministry.

This short paperback is written in a vigorous, forthright English style, to the point of being unconventional. However it is clear and read able.

Mr Clarke argues that church elder-ship should be male. He states the familiar arguments from Scripture and he also quotes many passages from the Bible which speak of male leadership.

The book is one long appeal to Holy Writ as being the final word in matters related.

He has no patience with those who argue that we must defer to modern opinion: "When men find themselves looking over their shoulders wondering what will this person or that person think of me if I do not do or say the approved thing then that is where Satan has got you. If you find your self not doing things which you know are right before God and proper because you feel others may disapprove of you, then that is Satan ensnaring you so that you will be ineffectual in your work for God'. **We are told to resist the Devil** and he will flee from you. (Page 76).

Much of the book is occupied with an exchange of letters between the author and the elders of Mr Clarke's church who have decided to appoint women elders.

He then enters into correspondence with the head of a Bible College who comes to Mr Clarke's church as a visiting preacher. These vigorous debates enable Mr Clarke to present his arguments in an interesting context. We recommend the book. Dr Napier Malcolm, editor of the British Church News Paper.

Contents

6

8

10

Authors Preface

I felt compelled to write this book, after my return from a 10 month preaching mission to the jails in the Philippines, between October 2002 and June 2003. The complete mission is recorded in my book , <u>Before The Cock Crows</u> which is the daily diary of that mission that was called Trojan Horse Mission to the Philippines.

Like all that I have written and published it is from my personal experience as a Christian, were I record those conflicts that I faced when seeking to follow Christ through the many difficulties that I encountered. I seek to show how the Lord stood by me when men forsook me. My desire is to pass on my learning to others .

My story of conversion from crime to Christ is told in my book, <u>Converted on LSD Trip</u> and also<u> Bierton Strict and Particular Baptists</u> and Borstal Boys, a book specially written for prison inmates in the UK. And now written as a punk rock opera, called <u>Borstal Boy,</u> seeking to tell this story to prison inmates and any other interested party.

I was converted and became a Christian on the 16th January 1970, and sought to followed Jesus Christ as best I could. I learned to read in order to educate myself.

I was not brought up in a Christian home nor connected with any church but learned the truths of the gospel of Jesus Christ through reading the bible and classical Christian literature my self.

Within three years of my conversion I came from ignorance, having no educational qualifications, and barely able to read. I had left school at the age of 15 years old, not knowing what the book of the Acts of the Apostles was all about, or why Jesus had to die, to a comprehensive knowledge and history of the bible; who Jesus is, the doctrines of grace, predestination, election, justification by faith, in short the historic teachings of the protestant reformation. These truths assisted me in my reformation turning from a life of crime to Christ.

In my earlier books I tell how I educated my self, went on to Higher Education, became a Baptist minister in a Strict and Particular Baptist church and taught electronics for over 20 years, in colleges of Higher and Further Education.

A Disappointment

In the Philippines I discovered sadly, to my disappointment, that many religious errors, in practice and doctrine had developed in a country, which is very religious. I had already encountered the beginnings of such errors some 20 years earlier when the I was a minister amongst Strict and Particular

Baptists in England. These errors include the failure to understand or the rejection of the facts that:

1   That the scripture both Old and New Testaments are the only source of reliable knowledge relating to the way of salvation.

2   That the underlying text of the New Testament are those manuscripts contained in the Majority or Received Text of Scripture, all of which were used by the Protestant Reformers.

3   That the New Testament epistles of the Apostles carry authority and are the word of God.

4   The Protestant Reformers correctly understand the way of salvation that is outlined and referred to by some as Calvinism.

Plenty of Religion

In the Philippines there was plenty of religion, a show of religion in statues and names and pictures that amounted to idolatry and superstition.

There was a striking difference between rich and poor even among the professed Christians. How ever it was in New Bilibid Prison, the National Penitentuary of the Philippines that I noticed and identified the problem of women elders who were called Pastora's that I seek to write about.

New Bilibid Prison Maximum Compound, housed over 13,000 inmates with 1200 men on Death Row. It was like a small town enclosing a microcosmic subculture of the nation and that reflected life in the fee society.

Within that compound was whole range of religious groups holding various differing religious beliefs and it was here we sought to teach the gospel as we had found written in the bible and had experienced first hand.

2 Introduction

The provocative question, "Does the Lord Jesus want women to rule as elders in His church", is a very reasonable one as we are living in the days of The Modern Woman, and women are being appointed as elders, leaders and preachers in the church. It never use to be so. I believe this provocative question will be the means of addressing the knew jerk reaction of the Modern Woman who objects to a woman's role in a Christian culture and also other matters they object too that scripture gives clear direction. I do not believe appointing women as elders honours women kind. Women do not respect men who are a weak, cowardly, or ineffectual persons.

Women Rights, Equality of Sex or Race

When treating the subject of women elders in the church we are not dealing with the affairs of a secular society and so it had nothing to do with women's rights, equality of sex or race in the world. This matter only relates to men and women in a Christian church. It is about the rules of the house of God, which is the church of the living God and rules for those who are members of the body of Christ and members of an heavenly county.

The Suffragettes

Emmeline Pankhurst 1858 -1928) was a Suffragette and worked very hard to bring equal rights for women to vote as men. In the year of her death all women over 21 gained the right to vote. The Suffragette movement brought about many changes for the better in a secular society but not so for women seeking to follow Christian principles. One of her famous quotes was, "Trust in God She shall provide". Terms which do reflect Christian beliefs. We know God will provide and He is not a she.

Further Consideration

Upon further consideration it is realised that we are looking at practical rules for Christian moral conduct with in the family, church and society . The Apostles of Christ taught that children should obey their parents in the Lord.

Ephesians 6. 1

Husbands should love their wives.

Ephesians 5.25

Marriage is between one man and one woman

Please see the section on, "Christian View of Marriage".

Matthew 19.5

The head of the woman is the man

1 Corinthians 11:3

Men should treat younger women as sisters and elder women as mothers.

1 Tim 5:2

We should pray for those in government. Give honour to where it is due.

1 Tim 2:2

Servants be subject to your masters , not only to the good and gentle but also to the froward.

1 Peter 2:18

They also speak of sexual moral conduct.

Rom 1:26

I have observed that Homosexuality and Female Elders go hand in hand.

Youtube Videos

Homo Sexuality and Women Elders

https://www.youtube.com/watch?v=xkTPPifWQgo

Same Sex Marriage
https://www.youtube.com/watch?v=cuuL4atvKsI

Suffragettes
https://www.youtube.com/watch?v=KKR_JtzwOkc

Women Elders Preterists
https://www.youtube.com/watch?v=mn5PzpVh0ek

Ancient Land Marks
We are taught is scripture not to remove the ancient boundary stones set up by our fathers; and in this case we are dealing metaphorically with doctrinal, moral and practical rules of conduct.
Proverbs 22:28
The Apostles speak of the conduct of men and women in the church environment giving clear instructions relating to the qualifications to be an elder in a Christian church.

And my view is that if we wish to follow Christ we must follow the teachings of the Apostles of Christ.

Weapons Formed Against Christians
This book seeks to show what the bible has to say about the role of women in the church and family. Since these rules are taught by the Apostles of Christ they are the word of God to us and we should obey. The secular world my differ and turn from the narrow path taught them in scripture but we should follow the word of God, this is our wisdom.

Our Citizenship
We that are Christian belong to Christ, our citizenship is in a kingdom that is not of this world. The Lord Jesus Christ redeemed his church, bought them with his blood, he gave his life and died for her. We are not our own we were bought with a price. The Church is his bride and he is her head. We are subject to Christ under His law. The church consists of believers who follow the teaching of the apostles of Christ. They are normally baptised, having been born again and receive the bible as the word of God. All instructions regarding doctrine, behaviour and practice are directions for believers and not directed at unbelievers who are not members of Christ

Mark Those Who Cause Division
We are exhorted by the Apostle Paul to "Mark those who cause division and offences", in the church, and avoid them.

Romans 16:17

I am writing this book to bring attention to the fact that certain men in the church where I attended in 1999 caused a division by seeking to promote women as elders. The church is the "Jesus Is Lord Church", Warsash, Hampshire UK.

I have mark and named the elders who caused the division with a view to point out the errors and contend earnestly for the faith once delivered to the saints.

Now I beseech you brethren mark them, which cause divisions and offences contrary to the doctrine, which ye have learned: and avoid them.

3 METHOD OF APPROACH

The following pages contain a documented history of this controversy that arose at the "Jesus is Lord" church. The controversy ended with my withdrawal from the church after they insisted I should remain silent and not object to a women being appointed as an elders.

I was asked "How could I continue to go to the Church if I hold such different views to them". I.e. I did not support them wishing to appoint women elders.

The History of The Elders Announcement

On the first Lord's day in January 1999, it was announced in church, by the church Secretary, that the elders were unanimous in their view that women could now be nominated to become elders in the church. I believed that this was wrong and contrary to scripture and was an error.

Documentary Evidence

This history is made known, by a series of letters and the correspondents between myself, the elders and other parties involved.

It was the elders who caused the division and so they were marked, according to the scripture. These men were responsible for the offence.

Please feel free comment and respond in any way you feel appropriate.

Martin Lloyd was the elder and the acting secretary, who responded to my complaint, on 25th January 1999 , after I questioned another elder about the proposition to opening up the rights of the church members to nominate women to the elder-ship.

4 MY REACTION TO THE ANNOUNCEMENT

When It was announce that church nominations were now open to women as well as men I immediately spoke to Brian one of the elders saying that I believed it wrong to appoint a woman as an elder, as it was contrary to scripture. I felt compelled to address this matter as it was introducing a controversy, in the church that was against the word of God.

I Write To The Elders

I straight-way wrote this letter to the elders at Warsash church.

Dear Secretary and Elders,

It was announced today that the Elder-ship were in unanimous agreement that women could be ordained as elders as well as men and nominations would be taken from the church to appoint new elders.

I groaned immediately as I felt very sad that a controversial issue was being introduced to the church. I spoke to Brian and another elder. (Two of the elders were away) saying I believed that the elders were in serious error on this point and I believed it my duty to say this to them. I stated that I did not like controversy and would avoid it but this matter was thrust upon the church.

I said that unanimity did not make a matter right, as all the disciples of Jesus were unanimous when they forsook him. That did not make it right.

I commended them for standing against making practicing homosexuals elders but I could not do the same about this issue.

The secretary said they had looked at the issue and that was their viewpoint and I should be subject to their authority.

I said I was not arguing about their authority but I was under authority to Jesus and I felt it my responsibility to say to them how I felt and believed. I stated that I did not have to believe what they believed.

I asked them what did they think I should do about the issue which has been raised by them not me.

Apostle Exhortation

My immediate thoughts called to mind the apostle Paul's exhortation to Titus which was to ordain elders in every city.

Titus 1:5

He says, "If any be blameless, the husband of one wife, having faithful children not accused of riot or unruly etc..

Holding fast the faithful word as he hath been taught, that he may be able by sound doctrine both to exhort and convince the gainsayers.

The Elders To Be Men Not Women

I Timothy 5:1

Paul states that an Elder should not be rebuked but entreated as a father and the younger men as brethren.

The next verse states that elder women should be treated as mothers; the younger as sisters. In these two verses an elder is male there is no suggestion that an elder is a woman.

I understand the Hebrew word for elder is " zaqen" meaning old age -

bearded. Meaning male as in

Gen 50:7

The Hebrew word for elder women "gadol" meaning great as in

Gen 29:16

Paul writes to Timothy

1 Tim 3:1

Saying, If a man desire the office of a (bishop), he desires a good work. The word bishop is similar to overseer as used in

Acts 20:28

In this place it states the Holy Ghost made them overseers. These were men not women as later in

Acts 21:5

It says their wives and children came and kneeled down as they parted. Paul states

1 Tim 3:2

That a bishop must be blameless the husband of one wife. One that ruleth his own house having his children in subjection. If a man know not how to rule his own house how shall he take care of the church of God.

Here we are to understand the bishop or overseer is a man not a women.

The Apostle does make distinction between the man and the women and argues his point from scripture.

Men To Pray Women To Adorn Themselves

1 Tim 3:8

He says I will that men pray every where lifting up holy hands, without wrath and doubting.

In like manor also that women adorn themselves in modest apparel with shame faced ness and sobriety.

Adam was first formed then Eve.

Adam was not deceived but the women being deceived was in the transgression.

I do not wish to be controversial but I believe the clear light of scripture should direct us and we should not be wiser that what is written. Obedience to Gods Word is better that sacrifice. Remember what happened to king Saul. I believe it is against the word of God to ordain women as elders.

Yours Sincerely
in the Name of our Lord Jesus Christ

David Clarke
End.

Lessons From Scripture

My thoughts on reflection about this matter were that I had learned the gospel truths from reading the scriptures very early on within a few months after my conversion from crime to Christ. I have written of my conversion and experience in my book, "Converted on LSD Trip", also "Bierton Strict and Particular Baptists" and "Borstal Boys". I was shocked that these men and elders wished to contradict and go against scripture.

A Letter of Reply

I received a reply to my letter from Martin Lloyd, which is as follows and I would like you to read carefully as it is importance for you to see where he is going wrong.

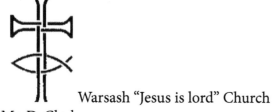 Warsash "Jesus is lord" Church

Mr. D. Clark
11 Hayling Close,
Fareham
Hants.

Warsash United Reformed Church
Interim Secretary: M. Lloyd
8 Home Rule Road,
Locks Heath,
Southampton,
S031 6LG
Tel. (01489) 581009
25 Jan. 99

Dear David,

Thank you for sharing with Brian and myself your concerns about the possibility of our fellowship having female elders and for the letter you gave me Sunday evening concerning the same subject. I should perhaps point out that it is not a new view and there is within the fellowship a number of female elders and has been for a number of years. They are at this point non-serving but still Elders.

I hope you will agree that what we are talking about is in fact a matter of interpretation of the scripture. Within the Elder-ship at Warsash we hold different views on some doctrine. We believe that God has called us as Elders and therefore accept by His grace one another's view while possibly not agreeing with it. Which of us is right and which of us is wrong is not important, what is important is that we love and serve our Lord Jesus Christ to the best of our ability. I believe at Warsash that is what the Elders are doing.

We have in the past been side tracked on different issues, which have been raised by various circumstances. These issues have in my opinion, at best, slowed our progress as a church and, at worst, prevented us doing what God has called us to do. I agreed that doctrine and interpretation of the Holy Scriptures is important but if it slows us down or stops us reaching out, which is what we believe our Lord is calling us to do, then it can not be right. If our doctrine prevents us from working with other Christians then we must throw it away and reconsider it. Doctrine has evolved over the years and praise God will continue to do so. No one has a pure doctrine and no one is perfect only Jesus.

Be assured that we will continue to pray over this and many other issues, and we thank you again for expressing your opinions and beliefs. Thank God that He has given us a fellowship in which we may do this openly.

Yours in our Lord Jesus Christ,
Martin Lloyd.

5 MY SECOND LETTER TO THE ELDERS

At first sight the response of Martin Lloyd might seem very reasonable and a kind considerate letter but that it not the case and felt it important to respond with reason and scripture to is reply and so here is my letter to him.

My letter of Response

28th January 1999

Dear Secretary and Elders,
Thank you for your reply to my letter regarding women elders.

I do not agree with you that the possibility of an appointment of women Elders at the Church is a question about interpretation of scripture.

I have declared to you what the scripture actually says about the appointment of Elders. I have not made any interpretation of the scripture but taken it in its literal straightforward sense.

Scripture is clear that men were to be appointed as elders in the church and not women. We have no example of a women being appointed as an Elder in the New Testament.

I have said I believe it a serious error to depart from the scripture revelation in this matter.

You say that you agree doctrine and the interpretation of scripture is important but if it slows us down or stops us reaching out then it cannot be right.

I believe this is also an error because the scripture says
2 Tim 3:16

All scripture is given by inspiration of God and is profitable for reproof, for correction, for instruction, in righteousness; that the man of God may be perfect, thoroughly furnished unto all good works.

On this basis I put to you that scripture teaches we should keep the commandments of God and not rush ahead because we want to make haste. This was the error of King Saul.

The scripture clearly tells us
1 Sam 13:12

of King Saul who rushed ahead of God, he did not want to be slowed down, and made his own burnt offering and supplication without waiting for the appointed priest of God. He felt he could not wait for Samuel. Verse 13 Samuel said to him you have done foolishly: thou hast not kept the commandment of the Lord.

We are also instructed by scripture to lay hands on no man suddenly
1 Tim 5:22

This is in the chapter where Paul instructs Timothy in the appointment of Elders.

I use the scripture here, in both places lawfully, to correct an error.

I believe it also another error to teach that the doctrine of scripture is progressive. The scripture is clear
Jude 3

that faith was once delivered unto the saints. This is not a progression but a revelation to the church, now contained in the scripture.

I grant that we grow in grace and the knowledge of Jesus Christ and so the doctrine of Christ. This is progressive but the doctrine of the gospel was delivered once unto the saints. There can be no new revelation about Elders to the church. The doctrine of Elders is contained in the scriptures alone, not in new revelation to the church.

I feel and sense that God is about to try or prove the church over this issue as He indicates He will do.

I am responding as I am instructed too
1 Th 5 19:21

to prove all things and to abstain from all appearance of evil.

The scripture teaches

Deut 13:1-3

Thou shall not harken to the voice of that prophet, or that dreamer of dreams: for the Lord your God proveth you to know whether you love the Lord your God with all your heart and with all your soul.

I believe I have done as I am called of God to do. To speak as I have so learned Christ.

I have no desire to be involved in contention or arguments. I would exhort you as I would a Father and a brother to hear what I say because I believe I speak the words of our Lord Jesus Christ in sincerity and truth.

Yours in the name of The Lord Jesus Christ,

David Clarke

28/1/99.

6 CHRIST FOR THE NATIONS BIBLE COLLEGE

About this time I was invited (30/01/1999) , as a potential student, to All Nations Bible College so I went to the open day early 1999.

The Dean Of Faculty was Charles Daniel who was known to the church at Warsash and also a visiting preacher. Whilst there I took the liberty to speak to the him about the issue of women elders as he was responsible for the subject of Biblical Authority at the bible college. He said he would have to have a Word from the Lord before appointing a women elder however she would have to have the appropriate qualifications. He was not against the principle of a woman elder.

I was disappointed at this reply as this meant I judged such teaching unsound and wanted to know the Bible colleges position before I considered any more being a student there.

Then Charles came and spoke to the Church at Warsash a week later and I report on his sermon shortly.

I Write To The Bible College

I wanted to speak to the Principle about the college's view on the subject of women elders but judged it best to write to him. Here is my letter:

8/2/99

Dear Mr. Swadling,

Thank you for your letter regarding the bible college training centre. I was very pleased to visit you on your open day and as a new potential student I found what you had to say very remarkable and helpful.

I wanted to ask about the colleges position regarding Female Elders as the church (name withheld URC) from whom I have received much help from have recently announced that the elders were unanimous in accepting women may serve as Elders in the church.

This has been very disturbing to me as the scriptures are clear that the qualifications for an elder is to be the husband of one wife and to have his children in all subjection.

There are no examples of women elders in the New Testament. The scripture speak against woman usurping authority over the man.

Peter Jacob, one of our former elders, taught use to speak and believe only what the scripture says. To reject every thing else.

The view held now by the elders is a deviation from scripture and has cause much distress and one family has now left.

In speaking upon the subject I was informed that the bible college shares the same view; that women may serve as elders in a Christian church.

I would be very grateful if you would speak clearly about the bible college position with respect to women elders.

Yours very sincerely

David Clarke.

Please share this with the Dean (visiting preacher) and your staff as I did speak to him briefly about the matter on the 30/1/99.

The Principals Reply

To: Mr D Clarke

11 Hayling Close

Fareham

Hampshire

P014 3AE

10th February 1999

Dear David

Thank you for your letter dated 8th February and I am pleased you enjoyed your time here at Christ For The Nations Bible Training College.

I note your question about Female Elders and really to clarify the situation I would say that Christ For The Nations does not officially have an opinion or view on this particular subject because we are not a Church and we teach about leadership. This sort of issue really is down to the individual Church Elders and leaders of the various Churches. I have photocopied an article, which Barbara Sambrooks, one of our lecturers here, has written which I think you should find quite helpful.

Also when we look back in history we see that God has very clearly used many women to become leaders and Elders in various denominations who have really been effective in the Body of Christ. I think what we have to do is look at the cultural background at the time for when Paul was writing to Timothy in the Scriptures you are quoting from Paul was talking to Timothy about the Church in Ephesus and it was a Jewish culture he was talking about and in the Jewish and Greek culture at that time men did have positions of authority and leadership but women seldom did.

There are many instances as you can see from Barbara's notes where women have been Church leaders and house group leaders and God has used them mightily. My personal opinion is if God anoints and calls someone then it is not up to us to judge and be divisive. It caused a great split in the Anglican Church but as far as l am concerned what is more important is not whether someone is male or female but rather their character and whether they are people of integrity or not? If you look at the qualifications of leadership in every part of the Bible what God is looking for is people whose heart is towards Him and that they obey what He is calling them to do. The Church I attend, The Vine Christian Fellowship actually has women Elders as well and I personally do not have a problem with that providing that as with men Elders they are people under authority: i.e. Submitted one to another.

I say these things are down to the individuals and in any Church situation if you belong to a Church and the leadership is doing things, which you feel, are not Scriptural and not right then obviously it is your choice to find a Church where you do fit and you are content and happy. In the broader context of The Body of Christ we should not judge one another and as I have said before as Christ For The Nations is not a Church we do not have to take a view on this other than try to give a balanced overall picture and various denominations and Churches come to their own conclusions.

I hope this has been helpful and if you would like to come and chat with me I would be more than pleased to do that.

Every blessing and hope to see you soon.

Kevin Swadling
Principal/Director
CHRIST FOR THE NATIONS UK DODSELY LANE EASTBOURNE
MIDHURST WEST SUSSEX GU29 OAD
TEL: 01730 817775 FAX: 01730 817992 E-MAIL
cfnuk@aol.com
CHRIST FOR THE NATIONS UK IS A REGISTERED CHARITY TRUST
No. 1064962

7 MY RESPONSE TO THE PRINCIPALS LETTER

The Principal acknowledged that the bible college has no official position as to whether a woman could be an elder yet they teach about leadership. I was hoping to hear the Word of God directs them in all issues like this and so we do not teach a women can be elders in Christian church.

He went on to give his personal view that history has dictated to him that it is OK for women to become Elders and they are very effective.

I realized that this was another serious error. We should never look to history for direction when God has spoke directly on the subject in question. If you look at history then look to Eve in the garden of Eden, **Gen 3. 16.** Do not take Eve as the example to follow suit. History teaches it is foolish to go against what God had spoken about. If we chose to go against what God as commanded we are wrong.

In his opinion the Apostle Paul's argument against women teaching and ruling was a cultural issue of his day and does not now apply to the churches of today.

This is another serious error. The Apostle argues in Corinth," if any wish to be contentious (regarding women acting in the church) we have no such custom, neither in the Churches" .

Cor 16

That is in the churches of the New Testament, not just Ephesus.

And again," Let your women keep silence in the Churches: for they are not permitted to speak; but they are commanded to be under obedience, as also saith the law

1 Cor14:3-4

That is not just Ephesus.

Other Apostolic Witnesses

And Peter states " Likewise ye wives be in subjection to you own husbands

1 Pet 3:1

This is Peter and not just Paul.

I have quoted from two Apostle who are witnesses to show that it is not a cultural thing but the way God had ordered things.

Kevin argues that if God anoints anyone to do any work in the church who are we to judge on the basis of sex.

I argue that it is not for me to judge what God orders or does and we are given the scriptures in order for us see the way and to, "try them that say they are apostles and are not". The church at Ephesus was commended by the Lord Jesus for doing just that.

Rev 2:2

The scriptures forbids women elders (and gives its reasons - these are creational not cultural reasons and the result of the fall) who are we to go against the Lord?

Kevin then gives example of The Vine Fellowship who have women Elders.

I thought it was a poor answer to sight the Vine Church has women elders. It is like Eve saying "Adam look I have taken the forbidden fruit and it looks good, tastes good and I'm sure it will do you good, Go ahead and eat it like me".

Resist the devil

The answer is no, we do not follow any man to do evil but resist evil and follow the Lord Himself.

I am told it is a local church affair and if I feel the local church is un-scriptural then I am free to go elsewhere.

Had Paul allowed Peter to oppose the Gospel, like he did, where would we be today. Paul contended earnestly for the faith once delivered to the saints he did not ignore problem but faced them and tackled them.

Not Alone In My Views

In order to show I am not self opinionated I requested the help of Dr. Ken Matto <kmatto@comcast.net>

Dr Ken Matto's answer to the Principals Reply

Kevin Swadling does not even quote one verse of Scripture to support his view about women elders and by answering the way he does becomes the authority by saying "my personal opinion." The fact that he has rejected the use of Scripture and the searching of it, suggests that he, like many has been feminized and is in Satan's camp. There are some other issues at stake when one elects to have women elders:

1) 1 Peter 3:1

(KJV) Likewise, ye wives, be in subjection to your own husbands; that, if any obey not the word, they also may without the word be won by the conversation of the wives;

Ephesians 5:24

(KJV) Therefore as the church is subject unto Christ, so let the wives be to their own husbands in every thing.

If you notice in these two verses, it speaks about the wife being subject to her own husband. If a woman is elected as an elder, then she has become a ruler in the church. She not only rules over her husband, but over every man in the congregation which is totally unbiblical as she is to be in subjection to her own husband. If she is an elder, then she also has the rule at home, for how can she rule her husband at church but not at home?

1 Timothy 5:17

(KJV) Let the elders that rule well be counted worthy of double honour, especially they who labour in the word and doctrine.

The word "elders" and "elder" in the New Testament, whether the elders of Israel or the elders of the church has 8 different inflections but they are all masculine gender except one which is in the feminine and it is the only place it is used in the NT.

1 Timothy 5:2

(KJV) The elder women as mothers; the younger as sisters, with all purity.

It is an adjective describing women who are elderly, not who are ruling as elders.

2) The second problem which arises is how can she be the husband of one wife?

Titus 1:5-6

(KJV) For this cause left I thee in Crete, that thou shouldest set in order the things that are wanting, and ordain elders in every city, as I had appointed thee: {6} If any be blameless, the husband of one wife, having faithful children not accused of riot or unruly.

She can be the wife of one husband but she cannot be the husband of one wife. That is an obvious prohibition for women elders.

3) If she insists on being an elder, then she plainly violates Scripture.

1 Timothy 2:12

(KJV) But I suffer not a woman to teach, nor to usurp authority over the man, but to be in silence.

She is not have authority over a man and if she is an elder, then she usurps authority over every man in the congregation, including her husband. She has now become the head of the house and has reversed God's order of authority. The word "authority" in the Greek is the word "authenteo" which carries with it the meaning of "have or exercise authority over." We already saw and it is as plain as day that elders have authority in the congregation

Dr. Ken Matto <kmatto@comcast.net> 15/03/2015

Women Can't Have Authority Or Teach

We shall now look at the article that Kevin Swadling sent me by Barbra Stanbrooks on the subject of women teachers and she was a teaching member of the staff at Christ For The Nations Bible College. Here is that article.

Barbara Sambrooks Article

Within 1 Timothy we have some very controversial verses of Scripture. It would be far easier to try to ignore them rather than explain them for fear of offending various groups within the Church.

We need to know something of the social background of Ephesus , the city where Timothy was a pastor the religious and social background has a great bearing on what was written

In Acts 19 we read that a riot broke out when Paul's preaching threatened the livelihood of the Silver Smiths who made idols of the goddess Artemis. The origins of this goddess went back far beyond the Greeks; she was the mother Goddess revered, in many guises, throughout Asia Minor. To the Greeks she was known as Artemis. The Romans knew her as Diana. In Graeco-Roman mythology, at the birth of Artemis/Diana, she was so horrified at the birth pains her mother endured that she was completely averse to marriage. In ancient writings praising the honour of Artemis she is portrayed as the one who remains a virgin, loves women, helps them to hunt and capture men in war, helps them in childbirth and even protects civil urban Greeks from the wild forest. She is seen as saviour and ruler of the cosmic powers. Astrology played an important role in her worship.

Ephesus housed Timothy's Church. It also housed the temple of Artemus. The Temple was the largest and most lavish structure in the whole of the then known world. It was used as a bank, money and valuables placed there were safe, no one would dare to violate the temple. The central object of worship in the temple appears to have been a meteorite called "Diopetes", which means "Fallen from heaven"

Acts 19:35

Priestesses attended the temple of Artemis. Males could only become priests if they had been castrated. These eunuch priests were called "Megabyzoi".

Another pagan religion that was prolific in Phrygia, the area in which Ephesus was situated, was the Cybele religion. Cybele was another "mother goddess". Again, any male priest in this religion had to be castrated. They were known as "Galli", they wore female clothing and let their hair grow like a woman's hair.

As we read through the epistles to Timothy we need to bear this background information in mind. Also, one must be aware that in the two pagan cults mentioned the women were dominant. With this short overview we can perhaps begin to appreciate the motivation behind Paul's writing.

The church in Ephesus, to which Timothy was the pastor, lived in the shadow of the great temple to Artemis. France writes that it "cannot have been unaffected by the surrounding atmosphere of a flamboyant and probably fairly uninhibited form of worship in which women and eunuchs played a leading role"(France p.58).

1 Tim 1

Timothy is urged not to let anyone teach false doctrines. It is interesting that "certain men" is more correctly translated "certain persons. Could it include women?

Why did Paul use an unusual term, why did he not use the plural of the word anthropos, or andros which both translate into the English as man?

I Tim. 1:7

Some people are wanting, to be teachers of the law but they have no understanding. If we keep the religious background in mind, and read this verse With Chp 2:11-12 we may gain a little more understanding of the text.

I Tim 2:12

"Authority" in the Greek text, a cognate of the word authento, is used. This only occurrence of this word in the whole of the New Testament, it does not even occur anywhere in the Greek version of the Old Testament. Authento is more correctly translated "usurped authority". It means to seize or assume power wrongly, to dominate Paul would not even let a man exercise "authento" within one of his congregations. Authority must be given, not grasped. Why would Paul have written such a thing?

If Paul had meant that a woman could have legitimate authority he could have used another Greek word, proistemi, which he has done in other places (Chp. 3:4-5,12, 5:17), and which is translated as authority, or management. The word he did use, authento, is used of one who does anything by his/her own hand. In non-biblical Greece it is used in regard to a murderer. What the women in the pagan cults, local to Ephesus, were doing was "murdering men", not physically but emotionally.

In the Syriac and Arabic versions of our Timothy text authento is understood to have connotations of insolence, bullying, domineering. One scholar has said that from the evidence it would seem that there were women in Ephesus who were brutalizing men.

Could it be that some female converts from the pagan religions had come into Timothy's congregation and were trying to have the superior role, as they would have had in the temple of Artemis? Such a background would certainly explain why such a large percentage or the letter contains so much about women. Here is Timothy, a young male leader in the Church, the equivalent of what would have been seen as a priest. In such a society as Ephesus it is no wonder that Paul wrote Chp.4: 12. We can see that Paul was writing to address the specific problems in Ephesus; other communities would not have had these same problems.

8 SALVATION THROUGH CHILDBIRTH

Does it mean that

1   A woman's salvation can be achieved through childbirth? What if a woman does not marry

2   Or does not have children, does it mean that she cannot be saved?

3   Does it mean that a woman will be kept safe through childbirth? . What of those thousands of women who die during childbirth?

If it is number three then the Word of God is untrue!

If it is either of the first two where is the place of the cross in the salvation process?

To exercise good exegesis we need to read Chp.2: 9-15). as a complete unit.

D.M. Scholer says that there was a problem in the church in that some women were despising their roles within marriage. This could be due to the local cults. (Chp. 1:9-1 I deals with women's dress and demeanor.

As we look at our section (2:9-1 5) this does appear to speaking about the marriage situation

Verse 12 Authority over a man (Gk. Andros). This verse, coupled with the rest of the section appears to be addressing marriage; Christian marriage. A women (Gr. Gune) can also mean a wife; there is no difference in Greek, just as andros can mean man or husband.

Paul then goes on to use the example of Adam and Eve, as France puts it; the paradigm married couple (vs. 13-14). Our section of the text concludes "with the commendation of childbearing, which is the most distinctive "wifely role". In the context of marriage it is the safest role if it functions within God's plan for the family (France p.61)

Vs. 13-15: The Explanation for these verses is often taken back to the creation principle. We read in Gen. 1 26-27 humankind, both male and female are given joint authority. This is a creation principle that human beings have authority. Authority is not based upon gender but upon who they are in relationship to their creator. Both male and female are created in the image of God and He delegated, or entrusted, authority to them. If we say that Adam, the male, was created first, then men have authority over women Then we have to conclude that priority in creation order would mean that humankind must be subject to the authority of the animal kingdom, which is nonsense. In Gen. chps.2 & 3 Adam was created first but Eve was first to get tempted. If the woman is responsible for sin's entry into the world why does Paul tell us that it was Adam (Rom.5)? (France p.67)

If Paul is saying, in Timothy, that women cannot he trusted with authority because they are more gullible surely such an argument can only be taken back to **Gen.3**. Here France suggests that this is an illustration of the potential dangers in relationships between men and women. In Gen. chps. 2 ~ 3 the woman took the initiative with disastrous consequences. She acted independently.

Nowhere in Paul's writing does he ever use, the word save with regard to physical safety, or well being. Christians are not guaranteed physical safety; Christ did not have it, Stephen did not have it, Peter did not have it, Paul did not have it we could continue. Can I draw your attention back to the religious background of Ephesus? Marriage was despised; childbearing was looked down upon in those pagan religions. Paul is trying to correct a perverted system of belief that had crept into the Church from the surrounding religious thinking. He wants Timothy to teach the wholesomeness of Christian marriage and family life. Remember that Artemis was the one who looked after women in childbirth. Paul is telling Timothy to teach that Christ will look after them in childbirth. Their salvation is secure in childbirth; whether they live or die their salvation is secure.

Main Source Books:

R.T France. Women in Church Ministry, Paternoster Press, Stambaugh & Balch.

The Social World of the First Christians, SPCK.

Barbra Sambrooks MA, BA., Dip. Th. Lecturer in Biblical Studies CFN UK.

A Disappointing Reply

From the Principals reply I was very disappointed and I sighed at the situation. Barbara Sambrook's article may be answered but that is not the object of my notes today. How ever here is my first response..

In the book of Revelation Ephesus is the first Church Jesus sent word too with a commendation because they could no bear them that are evil and who tried them who claimed to be Apostles and found them liars. They had laboured patiently and not fainted for the cause and name of Jesus Christ in the city of Ephesus and suffered persecution at the hands of

Rev. 2. 2

2 I know thy works, and thy labour, and thy patience, and how thou canst not bear them which are evil: and thou hast tried them which say they are apostles, and are not, and hast found them liars:

3 And hast borne, and hast patience, and for my name's sake hast laboured, and hast not fainted.

Ephesians 1

1 Paul, an apostle of Jesus Christ by the will of God, to the saints which are at Ephesus, and to the faithful in Christ Jesus:

2 Grace be to you, and peace, from God our Father, and from the Lord Jesus Christ.

3 Blessed be the God and Father of our Lord Jesus Christ, who hath blessed us with all spiritual blessings in heavenly places in Christ:

4 According as he hath chosen us in him before the foundation of the world, that we should be holy and without blame before him in love:

5 Having predestinated us unto the adoption of children by Jesus Christ to himself, according to the good pleasure of his will,

6 To the praise of the glory of his grace, wherein he hath made us accepted in the beloved .

7 In whom we have redemption through his blood, the forgiveness of sins, according to the riches of his grace;

8 Wherein he hath abounded toward us in all wisdom and prudence;

9 Having made known unto us the mystery of his will, according to his good pleasure which he hath purposed in himself:

Timothy Not A Weak Man

Timothy was not a weak man and contended earnestly for the faith once delivered to the saints and taught the sovereignty of God, predestination, election, particular redemption and church order, which included the distinctive roles of men and women in the church. The women were subject to their own husbands, prayed with their heads covered and kept silent in the church. It is my observation that those Christians who fail to teach these gospel truth fall away and adopt the view that women can be elders.

There would have been no trial of any woman in the church at Ephesus who claimed she was an apostle as that would never had arisen because it was forbidden for any woman to preach teach or usurp authority over the man. Any women could not claim to be an apostle for it was forbidden for a women to teach and usurp authority over a man. Had a woman tried to claims she was an apostle she would have been rejected as a liar , as other men were.

Diana and Artemis

The notable thing about Babrah Stambrooke article is that she is speaking about the role of women as teachers and having authority in the church. In her reference to the Temple of Diana and Artimas and the silversmith, who opposed the teaching of the Apostles, she outlines the prominence of the Goddess Dinah. She cites the legend that Artimas was horrified at the sufferings of her mother in childbearing. She now she had become a deity and all men serving in the temple of Diana were castrated. This sounds like a distortion of the historic facts relating to Eve in the garden of Eden.

It is written that God not only cursed the ground for mans sake but spoke to Eve saying because you have done this in pain you shall suffer in Childbearing. That her desire shall be towards he husband however he should rule over her.

In other words as the result of the sin of Adam and Eve in the garden God turned them out of the garden, cursed the ground so Adam would have to work by the sweat of his brow, Eve would now suffer in childbearing and she would have a natural desire to rule her husband but he would rule over her. This was some thing that God brought about.

Unto the serpent God said he would put enmity between his seed and the seed of the woman and it should brush his head and it should brush his heal. In other words this was a prophecy relating to how redemption would come about namely though the seed of the woman bearing the child, the Son of God, whose heal was bruised at the crucifixion but this was to crush the head of Satan.

So in the Christian community the gospel speaks about the relationship between man and woman, children and parents and man and women's role in the Church. Children are to be obedient to their parents, the woman was not to rule the man, was not to teach or function as an elder and learn in silence in the church . Also this relationship between man and women is compared to the relationship between Christ and his church. Christ is the head of the church even as the man is head of the women. It is this social conduct that is to be recognized and lived out in the community that is living in the world. Such is the law of Christ .

Certain Men

Barbara now sights a reference to certain men creeping in unawares and the suggestion is that "certain men" could mean men or women. This is a quotation from Jude and not spoken about the Ephesian Church. The words "certain men" in the Greek is "tines anthropoi". The word "anthropos" is the generic term for man. Barbara's case does not hold water because both words for "certain men" in **Jude 4** are in the masculine gender. In fact, all usages of "anthropos" in the New Testament are in the masculine. So it cannot mean male or female, just male.

Dr. Ken Matto
Mar 6 at 11:40 PM 2015

However Timothy would have been full well aware that certain men had been foreordained to condemnation just as Pharaoh and Judas and other apostates were.

Jude 1:4

For there are certain men crept in unawares, who were before of old ordained to this condemnation, ungodly men, turning the grace of our God into lasciviousness, and denying the only Lord God, and our Lord Jesus Christ.

The New International Version

This reads for certain individuals, whose condemnation was written about long ago, have secretly slipped in among you. They are ungodly people, who pervert the grace of our God into a license for immorality and deny Jesus Christ our only Sovereign and Lord.

In this version the citation of this text of scripture is used to cast doubt on the use of the word men. It is not a quote for the Majority Text of scripture as found in the Authorized King James bible of Jude verse 4 but from the unreliable Sinaiticus Text brought forward by Wescott and Hort in 1844. This is not a fair argument to suggest that when ever the word man is used we are to take it to mean man or woman. The context dictates that it is a reference to a man or men plural and masculine.

My Early Experience

As I have mentioned I have written this book out of my experience and conflict with professing Christians. In my early days I had to read the scripture and Christians books my self to learn the essential truths for my self. I soon learned that is was essential to have a reliable accurate copy of the bible and it became my firm conviction and belief that the **Majority Text** or **Received Text** of the New Testament was the word God and the all those so called scholars, who used alternative texts, such as the Sinaiticus, and Vulgate Latin versions to compose their New Testament were in fact leading others in error. This citation of Barbara Sambrooke in the New International Version (N.I.V.) is just such a case. Like wise Jehovah's Witnesses do just the same, they produced their own New Testament from selecting parts of corrupt manuscripts to compose their New World Translation.

9 A COMMENTARY ON CHRISTIAN CONDUCT

Matthew Henry's Concise Commentary 2:8-15

Under the gospel, prayer is not to be confined to any one particular house of prayer, but men must pray every where. We must pray in our closets, pray in our families, pray at our meals, pray when we are on journeys, and pray in the solemn assemblies, whether more public or private. We must pray in charity; without wrath, or malice, or anger at any person. We must pray in faith, without doubting, and without disputing. Women who profess the Christian religion, must be modest in apparel, not affecting gaudiness, gaiety, or costliness. Good works are the best ornament; these are, in the sight of God, of great price. Modesty and neatness are more to be consulted in garments than elegance and fashion. And it would be well if the professors of serious godliness were wholly free from vanity in dress. They should spend more time and money in relieving the sick and distressed, than in decorating themselves and their children. To do this in a manner unsuitable to their rank in life, and their profession of godliness, is sinful. These are not trifles, but Divine commands. The best ornaments for professors of godliness, are good works. According to St. Paul, women are not allowed to be public teachers in the church; for teaching is an office of authority. But good women may and ought to teach their children at home the principles of true religion. Also, women must not think themselves excused from learning what is necessary to salvation, though they must not usurp authority. As woman was last in the creation, which is one reason for her subjection, so she was first in the transgression. But there is a word of comfort; that those who continue in sobriety, shall be saved in child-bearing, or with child-bearing, by the Messiah, who was born of a woman. And the especial sorrow to which the female sex is subject, should cause men to exercise their authority with much gentleness, tenderness, and affection.

Barbra and Kevin are Wrong

As you will see from my previous answers Barbara is wrong. The Ephesian situation was not a cultural issue with women. The issue against women in the Ephesian Church was common throughout out the whole world as the churches custom for head coverings for women was customary in all the churches.

Apostolic Reasons

The Apostles Paul and Peter give reasons from scripture as to why man was to rule and not women, these reasons were derived from the way God ordained things. The Lord made it that way.

The things on earth are after the order of things in heaven. Just like the tabernacle in the Old Testament. As there is order in the Godhead so there is order between man and women. The Father, Son and Holy Spirit are co equal divine persons yet the Lord Jesus Christ is subject to the Father in things pertaining to our redemption. The woman is subject to the man in relationship yet equal in persons to the man before God.

God created man and women , male and female create he them.

According to the heavenly pattern. Which means the relationships between man and women are creational and not cultural. The man and women were created to reflect this relationship, at that time yet to be revealed between Christ and His Church. Just as the head of Christ is God the Father, which has nothing to do with culture so the head of women, is man (1 Cor 11 3). Adam was created first and then the woman as a help-meet for him. Adam named all the creature eve was not involved. Adam was the head of women, from the beginning. This is the Apostles argument. It would be foolish to depart from God's way of things.

The Curse

Some thing else took place after the fall after Eve took the forbidden fruit.

Adam , Eve and the ground were cursed by God and that curse remains so long as women gives birth to children in pain and thorns and thistle grow on bushes.

Gen 3:8

8 And they heard the voice of the Lord God walking in the garden in the cool of the day: and Adam and his wife hid themselves from the presence of the Lord God amongst the trees of the garden. 9 And the Lord God called unto Adam, and said unto him, Where art thou? 10 And he said, I heard thy voice in the garden, and I was afraid, because I was naked; and I hid myself. 11 And he said, Who told thee that thou wast naked? Hast thou eaten of the tree, whereof I commanded thee that thou shouldest not eat? 12 And the man said, The woman whom thou gavest to be with me, she gave me of the tree, and I did eat. 13 And the Lord God said unto the woman, What is this that thou hast done? And the woman said, The serpent beguiled me, and I did eat. 14 And the Lord God said unto the serpent, Because thou hast done this, thou art cursed above all cattle, and above every beast of the field; upon thy belly shalt thou go, and dust shalt thou eat all the days of thy life: 15 and I will put enmity between thee and the woman, and between thy seed and her seed; it shall bruise thy head, and thou shalt bruise his heel. 16 Unto the woman he said, I will greatly multiply thy sorrow and thy conception; in sorrow thou shalt bring forth children; and thy desire shall be to thy husband, and he shall rule over thee. 17 And unto Adam he said, Because thou hast hearkened unto the voice of thy wife, and hast eaten of the tree, of which I commanded thee, saying, Thou shalt not eat of it: cursed is the ground for thy sake; in sorrow shalt thou eat of it all the days of thy life; 18 thorns also and thistles shall it bring forth to thee; and thou shalt eat the herb of the field; 19 in the sweat of thy face shalt thou eat bread, till

thou return unto the ground; for out of it wast thou taken: for dust thou art, and unto dust shalt thou return. 20 And Adam called his wife's name Eve; because she was the mother of all living. 21 Unto Adam also and to his wife did the Lord God make coats of skins, and clothed them.

Imputed Righteousness A Safe Covering

Adam and Eve made themselves a covering to hid their embarrassment and felt the need to hid from God when they felt his presence in the garden. It was God who stepped in and made the first animal sacrifice to make them coast of skin which we learn pointed to the righteousness of Christ.

Fallen Angels

We learn later in scripture of elect angels, those angels who are good angels, who never took part in the rebellion against God along with the devil and others called fallen angels.

The good angels never experienced the fall and knew nothing of sin, they were preserved in Christ, by predestination, from the fall and Christ is their head and Lord. The fallen angels who were in the rebellion were responsible for their own fall. There is no redemption provided of them and they are lost for ever.

The coats of skin, or covering provided by God, for Adam and Eve were an indication of the righteousness that God had provided for them in Christ and also for all who obey God from a principle of faith in Christ.

For further reading see John Bunyan's Testimony and Dr John Gill, extracts at the end of the this book.

The Principal, Keven Swadling, then came and preached at the Church at Wasash shortly afterwards and he reasserted his views on that occasion.

10 BEHIND THE SCENE

After my visit to the Christ For The Nation Bible College and my correspondence relating to women elders in the church, within two weeks of this issue arising certain things, it seemed too much of a coincidence that Charles the Dean of Faculty should preach a sermon at the Warsash church that indicated a collusion with the errors held and taught by the Warsash Elders. After listening to his sermon on, 14 February 1999, I realised I must write to him in order for him to clarify what he had said and taught. Here is my letter to him.

Letter to the Dean (visiting preacher)

From: David Clarke
Copy to: The Elders Jesus is Lord Church.
17th February 1999
Dear Charles

Re: Your sermon at the Church Sunday 14/2/99

You raised some issues, which I felt needed to be clarified on Sunday. It seems some of the things you were saying were ambiguous giving a double message. The secretary was moved to say he believed it was directly from the throne of God. I heard ambiguous things and would like clarification.

Joshua 1:2

The Lord spake unto Joshua son of nun, Moses' minister, saying.

Moses my servant is dead; now therefore arise, go over this Jordan, thou and all this people.

The essence of the message was Moses is dead you now have a new leader. Do not look back to Moses- God is to do new things.

Afterwards I questioned you re - new doctrine and the fact that God is to shack every thing so that old doctrine must be cast away to be replaces by new doctrine. You had refereed to old wines skins and new wine skins etc.. I wanted to establish what you actually meant so I asked you "What new doctrine has God revealed to the church today which was not known to the early church in the Apostles time". You replied you said no, no. I did not say new doctrine like that but our understanding of it is new to us. Why do I think there are over 2000 denominations. I said I accept that and people grew in knowledge and understanding but the truths and gospel doctrine had been once delivered to the saint in the early church by the apostles.

I established or understood that you did not teach new doctrine or expect it.

I asked this because of our situation at the church and its seems things are changing. Former elders have left and another is to leave shortly. The the remaining Elders have announced recently they are unanimous in believing there is no reason why a woman should not be appointed as an Elder.

I have written to them saying how disturbed I am because this is a departure from the clear teaching of scripture. The reply I received was unsatisfactory and contained other issues, which were also in error. To which I have written but so far I have had not further correspondence. There has been no communication with me about it since.

I was informed that "doctrine and the interpretation of scripture is important but if it slows us down or stops us reaching out then it cannot be right".

It was also put forward that "the doctrine of scripture is progressive" - a statement which I took exception too.

It should be maintained the doctrines of Christ, as revealed in the New Testament Scriptures, have been once revealed. The truth concerning salvation and the church etc.. were taught by the Apostles in the New Testament times. The scripture of the Old and New Testaments contain the doctrines taught and received by the church. We are not to look for new doctrines there are none. If any one teaches we have more light than the Apostles and so teach new doctrine and new things they are in error. To depart from the teachings of the Apostles is a departure from the truth.

In light of this I would like to reflect on your sermon.

Dead To The Law

Yes Moses is dead and every believer is dead to the law (which came by Moses) by their union and death with Jesus when he died. Our baptism portrays this. This is so that we might be married to another even Jesus our husband and saviour who has been raised from the dead.

The Passing Away Of The Old Covenant

The Law and its administration has been shaken and no longer stands. The destruction of Jerusalem in 70 AD gives a full stop to that declared reality.

The Perfect Law Of Liberty

The Perfect Law of liberty and ministration of the Spirit has taken its place. Our Jesus is exulted above all things. We enter into the benefit of these things only as we like Joshua do not "let the word of God not depart from us." For It is to be a light and a lamp for our feet. There will be no rest if we depart from the clear teaching of the Word of God.

Joshua A Type Of Christ

Joshua is indeed a type of Christ but Joshua of old did not give the people of God rest otherwise God would not have spoken of another rest yet to be entered into.

Heb 4

let us therefore labour to enter into that rest. This labour is the labour of faith, which we exercise when we rest in Christ when we believe.

I understood you to be saying now that Joshua is come (a new leader) God is going to do new things do not look back to Moses etc.. throw away all you old teaching and doctrines and receive the new things God is going to do. This sounded awkward in light of our situation at the church.

Elders Wish To Depart From Scripture

The new leaders at Warsash are now saying they want to depart from scripture and appoint Women elders. This is not what Joshua did but rather he was charged then to follow the Lord in every thing.

Joshua 1

This book of the Law shall not depart out of thy mouth; but Thou shalt meditate therein day and night , that thou mayest observe to do according too all that is written therein.:

Turn not from it to the right hand or the left. Etc..

God was only with Joshua whilst he stuck with his God. The charge to any leader would be the same.

The people said to Joshua, "All that thou commandant us we will do, and whitherso ever though sendest us we will go".

According as we harken unto Moses in all things , so we will hearken unto thee only the Lord thy God be with thee.

Joshua would not have fared very well if he said the moment he took office I am going to abolish circumcision because he agreed he saw no reason for it and besides it upset the women folk. He would not have got very far. The people followed Joshua because he followed the Lord. Joshua was a courageous man of God and we should follow suit.

Elders Have Departed From Truth

Our Elders have departed from the Scripture on this issue of women elders. It is not a question of interpretation of scripture. The scripture could not be plainer. An Elder is to be a man and the women not to usurp authority over the man. Paul says :

Cor 14 :37

If any man think himself to be a prophet, or spiritual then let him acknowledge that the things that I write are the commandments of the Lord.

A Ridiculous Proposition

To suggest Christians throw away all old teaching and doctrines because they are old and get ready to receive new things is ridiculous. We should not throw away the truth about:

1   The Person of Lord Jesus Christ. Or how we should function as a new testament church.

2   Or the confession of faith or beliefs on the back of All Nations Bible college handbook. Unless they can be proved untrue from the Scripture of the Old and New Testaments.

We Have Spoken Before

I know I have spoken to you about women elders before but the question regarding your sermon was to clarify your general principle.

It could be taken from what you said you support a departure from scripture with the coming of a new leadership because God had said he will "Shake the heavens and every thing under them", to establish new doctrines like women elders in the church.

This , I think you would agree , would not have come from the throne of God.

Your Sincerely,

David Clarke.

My Thoughts On Reflection

I felt that my letter was very reasonable and to the point and it also gave Charles feedback which any preacher would value but How ever not every one thought as I did and the following week I was instructed to see the elders at the Warash church after the Sunday morning meeting.

11 SUMMONED TO SEE THE ELDERS

28/2/99

Today was the day I was summoned to see the Elders regarding my objections to them supporting women becoming elders?

On the 21/2/99 I was asked to meet the elders after the morning meeting, on the 28/2/99. I met with the elders as agreed and we meet in the small room. The Elders were 5 elders one being the secretary.

I was informed by the secretary that they had not called me to discuss any issue with me about women elders but rather as what had happened was so very serious he wondered had I any Idea how serious it was.

He stated I had written to a visiting preacher from a bible college and I was very rude to him. This was out of order as I was undermining the leadership at Warsash 'Jesus is Lord church'.

Art Thou He That Troubleth Israel

His tone of voice and method of speech was such that he might just well have said, " Art thou he that troubleth Israel"

1 Kings 18:17

I replied I was sorry if I had cause any offence but I had not meant too.

However before I could say any more I was silenced by the secretary's retort he said, "No, No it has got nothing to do with offence".

I said well I couldn't say any more as I did not know what to say.

I was told by the secretary that I was out of order and how could I explain my writing such letters not only to the visiting preacher but also the Elders.

In trying to explain I started to say "I was invited to become a member and assumed--- but before I could finish I was stopped from speaking again the secretary him saying, "No, no, not any more. That invitation to become a member had been with drawn".

I was taken back by this and had to checked this out with him first of all by saying I did not know that as it was news to me. He then said as far as he was concerned he would not support me becoming a member now and only then added could not speak for the others. The other elders remained silent so I assumed they were unanimous in this view too.

I said, "well I had not been aware of this until now and sought to explain that I was acting in good faith and in a way that I thought right.

I said to the secretary that I had asked him and another elder before when I raised my objection at first, how did they want me to deal with the issue. At that time the secretary had said they were the Elders and I should be subject to them. I asked them to pray with me over the issue as I knew this matter could not be left and I wanted to act in wisdom and to honour God.

I followed my objection by a letter to the elders and received a reply.

The reply I received was unacceptable as it contained very serious errors so I wrote back pointing them out to them.

I explained my letter to the visiting preacher was between him and me and that I had given a copy to them as I was being open with them and not doing things in the dark or a corner.

I said I had no intention of arguing with them and I was not going too.

The secretary said why did I write again without saying anything new. Another asked me elder, "then why all these letters if I was not arguing".

I replied to the secretary and said I was not saying anything new because I was sticking to the one issue. Women do not qualify to be elders according to the Word of God.

I replied to the elder I wrote again by way of reply to secretary in order to point out the errors contained in their reply to me. I simple state they were wrong and gave the reasons.

I could have informed the secretary that, "Rebellion is as the sin of witchcraft, and stubbornness is as iniquity and Idolatry". That like King Saul who was instructed to go and smite Amalek and utterly destroy all that they have and spare them not; but slay both man and women, infant and suckling, ox and sheep camel and ass. They too have not obeyed the commandments of God.

God has instructed the church men are to be elders not women. They want to go beyond the commandants of God and appoint women contrary to the scriptures. Saul thought it a good thing to spare the best of the sheep and oxen, to sacrifice to the Lord their God. Saul did not obey the voice of the Lord but did evil in the sight of Lord.

1 Sam. 15:1-23

To go beyond scripture and against scripture is the same sin as King Saul.

I was then asked if I would subject my self to the elder ship should women join their team.

I replied it depends what they meant. I said they were not ruling my conscience and they had no jurisdiction over my faith. I said I would be subject to their authority in respect to the things in the church.

I also said I would not be saying any more to them about women elders.

I am In A Seriously Bad Way

The secretary told me that he had known me 5 years and as far as he could see I had not change in all that time. He saw no change in me and it saddened him very much. He stated I was seriously spiritually in a bad way. I replied to Martin that if that was the case then the Lord Jesus was sadder that him.

He said I was consumed with this women elder ship, that it had taken me over. He maintained no one writes pages the way I did on such a subject.

I replied to the secretary saying I am not the same as him. I was different. That he was now judging my motives. I explained this had not consumed me as I had far more serious and pressing things in my life to deal with at the moment. I thought to my self, after the event, that it was written of Jesus "the zeal of thine house has eaten me up".

Psalm 69:9

which of course is commendable.

The Elders recently in normal course of events brought up this issue, so I acted normally for me. The secretary then told me they could not help me. That he had already recommended some time ago I go to El El ministries.

I asked were they asking me to leave. The secretary said how could I continue going there if I held the views I held.

I suggested that if they thought I was wrong in this issue, why did they wish me to leave, as surely they would want me to come to know the truth and follow them. (This being the scripture reason for reproof)

I suggested by staying they could help me. I certainly would wish them to come to knowledge of the truth this was why I had written to them in the first instant, and this would be my wish for the future.

I went on to explain I had been helped this past year and blessed of God at the Church and I had no intentions of going elsewhere, at the moment. However I asked if they would support me if I looked elsewhere; another elder said they would.

I said I had no intention of going elsewhere nor was I making any threats. I also said had I known that they held to women being elders I would not have sought to join them when asked to do so

At that time there were six male elders and no hint a women becoming and elder. I said I would be looking elsewhere but at the moment I have no where else to go.

I reiterated I had acted out of love to them in dealing with this issue. I did not want to get involved in controversy. It causes me great distress. I did not want it but I did what I believed the Lord would have me do.

I had been faithful to the Lord Jesus.

I felt very calm and was not surprised at their reaction. I was very disappointed however and felt sad at such a situation.

They That Honour Me I Will Honour

I felt the Lord stood by me and I know I had been faithful to the Lord in this issue. I am reminded " They that honour me I will honour".

1 Sam 2:30

I now know how Paul felt when he wrote," no man stood with me, but all men forsook me.

2 Tim 4:6

End.

David Clarke: March 1999.

12 FORMER SUPPORT FROM THE CHURCH

Over the past year I had received a great deal of help and support from the church.

During this time there were seven male elders and there were no women elders and I understood these men were seeking to honour the Lord in every thing.

The churches had also decided to sever links with their trustees who were the United Reformed Church. This was because the trustees supported homosexuals becoming elders. The Warsash church did not support homosexuality. I supported them in their stand against homosexuality and encourage them in it.

In November I had been asked if I would like to become a church member and I said I would like too but I declined in the end, due to my domestic situation. I was informed I was to consider my self-one of the church and could join when I wanted.

After this one of the former elders announced he was leaving with his wife and also another senior elder announced he would also be leaving, in May 1999. Another former elder had also left leaving only five left. There had never been a mention of women being elders whist I was there. It was at this time these remaining elders sought to appoint new Elders and open up nominations for women. At my meeting with the elders it was stated that they saw no reason why a woman should not become an elder so felt it my duties to give the reasons. Now I had learned these things soon after I had become a Christian and was use to establishing every point of belief from scripture alone and this was what surprised me, why did these men not do so ?

Blindness No Excuse To Ignore Scripture

We see no reason why women should not be made elders is a quotation of the Elders at "Jesus is Lord Church" Warsash !

These are the scriptural reasons why women should not be made elders or rule over men .

Man is the head of the woman

1 Cor 11

But I would have you to know the head of every man is Christ; and the head of the women is the man and the head of Christ is God.

Every man praying of prophesying, having his head covered, dishonoureth his head.

But every women that prayeth or prophesieth with her head uncovered dishonoureth her head; for that is even all one as if she were shaven.

For if a women be not covered , let her also be shorn: but if it be a shame for a women to be shorn or shaven, let her be covered.

For a man indeed ought not to cover his head, for as much as he is in the image and glory of God, but the women is the glory of the man.

For the man is not of the women ; but the women of the man.

Neither was the man created for the women but the women for the man.

For this cause ought the women to have power on her head because of the angels.

Never the less neither is the man without the women , neither the women without the man in the Lord.

For as the woman is of the man , even so is the man also by the women; but all things are of God.

Judge in your selves: is it comely that a woman pray unto God uncovered.

Doth not even nature itself teach you , that if a man have long hair, it is a shame unto him ?

But if a woman have long hair it is a glory to her: for her hair is given her for a covering

If any man seem to be contentious , we have no such custom neither in the churches of God. (Either there were more than one church at Corinth or Paul means all the churches throughout the world)

Christian Practice

This was Christian practice and not a cultural practice from the world and the reason for it is because of what scriptures teaches regarding the relationship between the man and women in creation and since their fall into sin in the garden of Eden. A Christian marriage was to reflect the relationship between Christ and His church.

Adam Created First

God made Adam first giving him instructions and commandments to name the creature and not to eat of the tree of the knowledge of good and evil before Eve had been made.

Gen. 2

And the Lord God took the man and put him into the garden of Eden to dress it and to keep it.

And the Lord God commanded the man saying of every tree of the garden you may freely eat: but of the tree of the knowledge of good and evil thou shall not eat of it for in the day that thou eatest thereof thou shall surely die.

Adam Named The Creatures Not Eve

Gen. 2:19

And out of the ground the Lord God made every beast of the field and every fowl of the air; and brought them unto Adam to see what he would call them: and whatsoever Adam called every living creature , that was the name thereof.

And Adam gave names to all cattle, and to the fowl of the air, and to every beast of the field; but for Adam there was not found an help meet for him.

Eve A Helper

God made Eve for Adam in order to help and support him in his work

Gen. 2:18

And the Lord God caused a deep sleep to fall upon Adam and he slept: and he took one of his ribs, and closed up the flesh instead therof

And the rib which the Lord God had taken from man, made he a women, and brought her unto the man.

Subjection After The Fall

God placed women under subjection to man after she had sinned in the Garden of Eden. This is not a cultural issue.

Gen. 3:16

Unto the women he said, I will greatly multiply thy sorrow and thy conception; in sorrow thou shall bring forth children; and thy desire shall be to thy husband and he shall rule over thee.

Peter Instructs Wives To Be Subject To Their Husbands
Wives should be subject to their own husbands , says Peter the Apostle to the Jews.

1 Peter 3

Likewise ye wives be in subjection to you own husband; that if any obey not the word, they also may without the word be won by the conversation of the wives;

While they behold your chaste conversation coupled with fear.

Whose adorning let it not be that outward adorning of plaiting the hair and wearing of gold, or of putting on of apparel;

But let it be the hidden man of the heart in that which is not corruptible, even the ornament of a meek and quite spirit, which is in the sight of God of great price.

Examples From Scripture
For after this manor in the old time the holy women also who trusted in God, adorned themselves being in subjection to their own husbands:

Even as Sara obeyed Abraham calling him Lord: whose daughters ye are as long as you do well and are not afraid with any amazement.

Paul the Apostle to the Gentiles
Wives should be subject to their own husbands says Paul the Apostle to the Gentiles

Ephesians 5

Wives submit yourselves unto your own husbands, as unto the Lord

For the husband is head of the wife , even as Christ is head of the Church : and he is the saviour of the body.

Therefore as the church is subject unto Christ, so let the wives be to their own husbands in every thing.

Col. 3

Wives submit your selves unto your own husbands, as it is fit in the Lord.

Women To Learn In Silence
Women to learn in silence not to teach or usurp authority over man

1 Tim. 2:11

Let the women learn in silence with all subjection.

But I suffer not a women to teach, nor usurp authority over the man, but to be in silence.

For Adam was first formed then Eve.

And Adam was not deceived but the women being deceived was in the transgression.

Notwithstanding she shall be saved in childbearing, if they continue in faith and charity and holiness with sobriety.

This was the rule in all the churches not just Corinth

These are the commandments of the Lord not Paul's opinion

1 Cor 14:34

Let your women keep silence in the churches: for it is not permitted unto them to speak; but they are commanded to be under obedience, as also saith the Law.

And if they will learn anything, let them ask their husbands at home ; for it is a shame for a women to speak in the church.

If any man think himself to be a prophet, or spiritual then let him acknowledge that the things that I write are the commandments of the Lord.

Aged Women To Teach Younger Women

Tit. 2 1

The aged women likewise that they be in behaviour as becometh holiness, not false accusers, not given to much wine, teachers of good things; that they may teach the younger women to be sober to love their husbands, to love their children,

To be discreet, chaste, keepers at home, good, obedient to their own husbands, that the word of God be not blasphemed.

Elder-ship Men Not Women

Elders to be men not women ruling his own house well

Tim. 3

This is a true saying, if any man desire the office of a bishop (elder) he desires a good work.

A Bishop must be blameless, the husband of one wife, vigilant, sober, of good behaviour, given to hospitality, apt to teach;

Not given to wine no striker, not greedy for filthy lucre; but patient, not a brawler, nor covetous;

One that ruleth his own house, having his children in subjection with all gravity.

For if a man no not how to rule his own house, how shall he take care of the church of God ?

A Note Of Explanation On

Tim. 2

Notwithstanding she shall be saved in childbearing, if they continue in faith and charity and holiness with sobriety.

The word saved is the same word used to describe the experience of the women with an issue of blood for 12 years and Jesus healed her. She was made whole (saved).

Made whole = saved.

A women will find wholesomeness (saved) in child bearing. I.e. Bringing up children and functioning as a godly wife. God made her to love and support a husband and bring up children.

The Virtuous Women In Proverbs

Proverbs 30:10

Who can find a virtuous woman? For her price is far above rubies.

11 The heart of her husband does safely trust in her, so that he shall have no need of spoil.

The whole chapter treats of the fulfilled women.

These are some of the scriptures, which speak directly on the subject of women and leadership. I hope this is of some help. This matter is as clear as Jesus is Lord.

Man should protect women not help ruin them

Why do women wish to resist Gods order by wanting to become Elders? Men who support women in this area are not protecting them. When Eve sinned Adam should have prayed for her, not go along with her sin. So men ought to contend for the truth of God in this matter, to safe guard women from similar consequences. Other wise they will become Punget (Ugly)

A Warning To The People Of God

Isaiah 3

As for my people, children are their oppressors, and women rule over them. O my people they, which lead thee, cause thee to err, and destroy the way of thy paths.

Isaiah 8

To the Law and the testimony: if they speak not according to this word, it is because there is no light in them.

To ignore Gods word on a matter so plain is foolish. Should we ignore the Word of God it might even be written of us one day "Let them alone: they be blind leaders of the blind".

Matthew 15 4

I have given more than seven scriptural quotations to show that a woman cannot qualify to be an elder. I am however also aware it is written: the sluggard is wiser in his own conceit than seven men that can render a reason.

Prov. 26:16

I would urge you to reconsider the issue regarding women Elders. This is my duty to you all in love. I am speaking the Word of God in the name and authority of the Lord Jesus Christ. This is a trial to both you and me.

I certainly can see how the Lord tried me in this issue to see if I am prepared to speak out for Him.

David Clarke
16/2/99
Hayling Close,

13 A TRIED FAITH

It was after this battle with the elders at Warsash I decided not to attend their meetings any more but felt it right to write to the church and give them a copy of what I had written. I also wrote my views as to their future and how God works with men. Here were my thoughts.

The Lord is testing the "Jesus is Lord Church"meeting at Warsash
21st February 1999

The Trial Of Your Faith - God Will Try You

It may seem surprising to some that God tries our faith, to see if we love him or no, just as he tried Abraham and the children of Israel.

How these trials come to us it doesn't matter.

What matters is how we react to them and deal with them. We should be faithful to God in our trials; obedience to God is better than sacrifices.

Abraham An Example

Abraham was called of God to go to a land that God would show him.

God promised Abraham a son in his old age to be his heir

We read in Genesis

Gen. 15

After these things the Word of the Lord came unto Abraham in a vision saying, fear not Abram: I am thy shield, and exceeding great reward.

And Abram said Lord God what wilt thou give me, seeing I go childless and the steward of my house is this Eleazer of Damascus?

This shall not be thine heir but he that cometh forth out of thine own bowls shall be thine heir.

And he believed in the Lord and He counted it to him for righteousness.

God Tries Abraham's Faith 40 Years Later

Forty years after God had promised Abraham a son in his old age God tried Abraham so see if he feared the Lord.

Genesis 12

For now I know thou fearest God , seeing thou hast not held thy son, thine only son from me.

We read of Abraham's trial in

Genesis 22

And it came to pass after these things, that God did tempt Abraham, and said unto him, Abraham: and he said, behold here I am.

And he said Take now thy son, thine only son Isaac, whom thou lovest, and get thee into the land of Moriah; and offer him there for a burnt offering upon one of the mountains which I will tell thee of.

Abraham Obeyed God

Hebrews 11

By faith Abraham when he was tried offered up Isaac: and he that received the promises offered up his only begotten son.

God Proved Abraham To Be Faithful

Genesis 12

And he said lay not thine hand upon the lad, neither do thou any thing unto him: for now I know thou fearest God , seeing thou hast not held thy son, thine only son from me.

Abraham a pattern for believers

We too as believers will go through trials as Abraham did. We have the scriptures to support us and direct in these trials.

We Are Encourage To Withstand Trials

James 1

Blessed is the man that endureth temptation: for when he is tried, he shall receive the crown of life, which the Lord hath   promised to them that love him.

We All Shall Have Trials

1 Peter 1

That the trial of your faith , being much more precious than of gold that perisheth, though it be tried with fire, might be found unto praise and honour and glory at the appearing of Jesus Christ.

And in another place

James 1

My brethren count it all joy when ye fall into divers temptations;

Knowing this that the trying of your faith worketh patience.

Difficult Trials Are Those Sent By God

As the children of Israel were tried and tested those 40 years in the wilderness so will we be tried in the same way by God during our Christian life.

Deut 8

Moses said, "All the commandments which I command this day shall ye observe to do , that ye may live and multiply , and go in and posses the land which the Lord swore unto your fathers.

And thou shalt remember all the way which the Lord thy God led thee these forty years in the wilderness, to humble thee, and to prove thee, to know what was in thy heart, whether thou wouldest keep his commandments, or no".

As God lead them in the way to prove them and humble them to know what was in their heart so he will try us today. And He is doing so in just the same way.

Gods Trials Have A Purpose

God wishes us to be faithful to Him in everything. God will try us to see if we will be faithful to his word. His word is a lamp unto our feet.

It seems to me that the trial presented to us at the moment is the issue about women elders. This is a trial sent of God. It is to try us to know what is in our hearts. To see if we will keep His word or no.

I have spoken to the elders about the issue. I am told we are the Elders I should be subject to their authority. I am not questioning their authority but their wisdom.

I feel the Lord would have me speak about this issue openly . I am responsible to speak what the Lord has taught me

I have put together, in these papers, several scriptures pointing out Gods word to us on the issue about women elders. It is very clear. An Elder is to be a man, the husband of one wife, with his children in all subjection. Not a women.

I would ask you to read these scriptures on the subject and make you own minds up. I would exhort you to act according to the word of God.

We are told by the Lord Him self he will try us in issues like this

Deut. 13

If there Arise among you a prophet or dreamer of dreams and giveth you a sign or a wonder, and the sign or the wonder come to pass , whereof he spoke unto thee saying, let us go after other gods , which thou has not known , and let us serve them :

Thou shalt not harken unto that prophet , or that dreamer of dreams : for the Lord you God proveth you to know whether ye love the Lord your God with all your heart and with all your soul.

What Are We Going To Do - God Is Trying Us Today

It is my privilege to encourage you in the Lord your God. I have not been called hear to no purpose And is my delight to see Jesus honoured and gloried in our midst.

My desire is you prove true to the Lord in this trial and act the way the Lord wants you too.

I say follow Gods word which speaks clearly to us stating that a women does not qualify to be an elder.

14 CHRISTIAN MARRIAGE

This is published to help all who have been troubled by divorce and remarriageor wish to be married. It is also directly linked to the role of women and elders. For if we know the reason and purpose for our existence we may know how to function and for what and how to pray as we are instructed to do all things fro the glory of God.

1 Cor. 10.31

In the Beginning

God from the beginning of creation God instituted and defined marriage. There can be no same sex marriage.

Adam was made first and Eve was made from Adam's flesh and bone as his help-meet. After they had fallen into sin God spoke reprovingly to Adam for harkening to the voice of his wife after she had sinned in the Garden of Eden. God also spoke to the women saying,

Gen. 2:18

"I will greatly multiply thy sorrow and thy conception; in sorrow thou shalt bring forth children; and thy desire shall be to thy husband and he shall rule over thee ".

Gen. 3:17

To Adam he said because you have harkened to the voice of your wife and disobeyed my voice he cursed the ground saying in sorrow would he eat of it all the days of his life. Thorns and thistles would grow and in the sweat of his brow would he eat bread. Until he die.

As women suffer in childbirth and thorns and thistles grow and men have to work by the sweat of their brow so this curse remains and has not been removed because God uses this for his own glory.

Natural Disposition The Women To Rule

From these scriptures we learn that the natural disposition of the woman is a desire to rule over her man and this is part of the curse, but he must learn to rule over her. In the same way the Lord directed Cain.

Genesis 4:7

If thou doest well , shalt thou not be accepted? And if thou doest not well , sin lieth at the door. And unto thee shall be his desire, and thou shalt rule over him. As Cain was to rule over sin so Adam was to rule over his wife. We may learn from this and hearken to the voice of God.

New Testament Revelation

As we come to the New Testament we learn from the example of our

Lord Jesus Christ how to rule our wives and this is by love. For it is written he loved his Church and gave himself for her; so too must we love our wives. The women are not commanded to love their husband but rather to honour and respect them.

The Christian View Of Marriage Has Always Been Clear

Ephesians 5:2

" Wives submit yourselves unto your own husbands, as unto the Lord. For the husband is the head of the wife, even as Christ is head of the church: and he is the saviour of the body. Therefore as the church is subject unto Christ, so let the wives be subject to their own husband in every thing.

Husbands love you wives even as Christ loved the church and gave himself for it. Etc.. So ought men to love their wives as their own body. He that loveth his wife loveth himself.

For this cause shall a man leave his father and mother and shall be joined unto his wife, and they two shall be one flesh.

1 Cor. 12:3

Before God the head of every man is Christ and the head of the woman is the man and the head of Christ is God.

There is clarity about the position and roles of man and women before God.

In this light we can view marriage.

There is no direct indication in the scripture as to how a marriage is entered into but it is generally agreed that marriagel is a covenantal relationship and the man and woman wishing to marry undertake certain things.

Marriage promises are made in public before witnesses.

They must do this willingly

There is a leaving the parental home and a cleaving too each other. The Intention is for life

Partners cannot leave the marriage

A Marriage Can Only Be Devolved If

a   Adultery takes place and that only by the injured party. Divorce does not have to take place if adultery happens.

b   The unbelieving partner wishes to leave (this leaving being an act of the will and ceasing to behave as a married person) and the believer releases them.

The legal part to marriage and divorce is only a technical aspect. It is not the actuality. Just like a death certificate does not make the person dead nor a birth certificate give life to the baby, neither does a marriage or divorce certificate make a marriage or give rise to divorce.

Christian marriage involves the marriage partners promising each other certain things. The following marriage vows are derived from scripture and are long-standing Christian beliefs.

A   The man promises his bride to love, honour, cherish, care and look after her even as Christ loves and cares for his church.

Col 3:19, Eph 5:2 , 1 Pet 3:7

B   The women in return promises to love honour and obey her man (as the church does to Christ). This is the pattern spoken of in

Eph. 5:22-24

This order and pattern of promises are only derived from the scripture and has been the order of things throughout the Church age.

These promises form a covenant and they are made before God and in presence of witnesses. It is not a contract but a covenant and should not be broken. Even if partners fail to fulfil their promises. They are still bound by promise to fulfil their vows. Even if they ignore their vows they are still married. Each partner is responsible to go the second mile in making the relationship work.

In the marriage all the husband has is his wife's even his body and likewise all the wife has belongs to her husband.

This form of marriage is how God intends it to be and I would argue to depart for the scriptural view of marriage is to turn from what God has revealed. I cannot see how any one in their right mind would turn from Gods way of things.

David Clarke   21st Feb 1999

A Heavenly Pattern For Us On Earth

When God the Father set up Christ for our living head he gave us eternal life in him; as it is written, "In hope of eternal life, which God that cannot lie promised before the world began."

Titus 1:2

Christ is the head of all things to the Church, which is his body, the fulness of him that filleth all in all.

Eph. 1.23

Christ is the quickening Spirit, that quickens all his redeemed; for he is our life, who has brought life and immortality to light through the gospel. In another passage he himself saith, "Because I live ye shall live also."

John 14:19

And it must be so; "For, as in Adam all (his natural seed) die, even so in

Christ shall all (his spiritual seed) be made alive."

When Christ was set up he was appointed to be the husband of God's chosen daughter. And as man and wife they were viewed one in union from everlasting; for the covenant of grace is a covenant of eternal wedlock: as it is written, "A certain king made a marriage for his son."

Matt. 22:2

The covenant of wedlock runs like this, as God the Father speaks to his elect, "Thou shalt no more be termed Forsaken; neither shall thy land any more be termed Desolate; but thou shalt be called Hephzibah, and thy land Beulah; for the Lord delighteth in thee, and thy land shall be married. For as a young, man marrieth a virgin, so shall thy sons marry thee: and as the bridegroom rejoiceth over the bride, so shall thy God rejoice over thee."

Isa. 62:4,5

Thus the elect were chosen as the king's daughter-in-law from eternity."

Ps. 132:13

They are espoused in time;

2 Cor. 11:2

and the marriage shall be consummated in bliss, when the mystery of God is finished; as it is written, "Let us be glad and rejoice, and give honour to him; for the marriage of the Lamb is come, and his wife hath made herself ready."

Rev. 19:7

And then she shall be clad in gold of Ophir, and be brought with joy and rejoicing to enter into the king's palace.

Ps. 45:15

Our Life Was Hid With Christ In God

This mystery was exhibited by Eve's existing in Adam before she was extracted from him; so our life was hid with Christ in God. And, when Eve was taken out of Adam, she was a help-meet formed for him; so the elect are created anew in Christ Jesus. When Eve was formed, God brought her to Adam; so no man can come to Christ except the Father draw him. When she came to Adam he received her as God's gift; so the elect are given to Christ. Adam and Eve are said to be one; so also are they that are joined to the Lord one spirit. Adam said, "Man shall leave, his father and his mother, and shall cleave to his wife;" so Christ came forth from the Father, leaping upon the mountains. And, when some of the Saviour's followers said. "Behold, thy mother and thy brethren stand without, desiring to speak with thee; he answered, Who is my mother and my brethren? And he stretched out his hands towards his disciples, and said, Behold my mother and my brethren!"

Matt. 12:47,48

Thus Christ left his father and mother, and clave to his wife. Adam had one wife brought to him and no more: so Christ says "There are threescore queens, and fourscore concubines, and virgins without number; my undefiled is but one."

Song 6:8,9

When Eve fell Adam was in the transgression, though he was not deceived; so when the elected spouse fell, Christ was not deceived, yet he was made sin, "and was numbered with the transgressors."

Isa. 53:12

When Adam and Eve fell, their marriage was not made void; so the fall of the elect did not break the bond of God's everlasting covenant, but rather paved the way to display eternal love towards the miserable. It appears that both Adam and Eve were chosen vessels; and, when they fell by eating the apples, they fell into soul travail, and were shortly after born again. Eternal love raised them up under the same tree where they fell; as it is written, "I raised thee up under the apple tree: there thy mother brought thee forth, there she brought thee forth, that bare thee."

Song 8:5

This mother (according to Paul) Is the heavenly Jerusalem;

Gal 4:24

And the heavenly Jerusalem; is the covenant of grace and God's elect in it; both typified by Sarah and her son Isaac. To Adam and Eve was the first promise of the covenant of grace revealed; and by the application of the promise were they brought forth from black despair to hope in God's mercy through Christ.

A Great Mystery Christ And the Church

I shall conclude this head with the apostle's mystery, "For no man ever yet hated his own flesh; but nourisheth and cherisheth it, even as the Lord the church. For we are members of his body, of his flesh, and of his bones. For this cause shall a man leave his father and mother, and shall be joined unto his wife; and they two shall be one flesh. This is a great mystery; but I speak concerning Christ and the Church."

Eph. 5:29-32

This therefore is another blessed effect of God's everlasting love. But, as a surety Christ was set up from everlasting; as it is written, "But Christ was made with an oath by him that said unto him The Lord swore, and will not repent, Thou art a priest for ever after the order of Melchisedec. By so much was Jesus made a surety of a better testament."

Heb. 7:21,22

First, Christ, as a surety, was to pay the debt of perfect obedience to the perceptive part of the law for his elect; as it is written, "He will magnify the law, and make it honourable."

Isa. 42:21

"So by the obedience of one (Jesus Christ) shall many be made righteous."

Rom. 5:19

As a surety, he was to pay the penal sum of suffering for his elect, by dying in their room and stead; as it is written, "I will ransom them from the power of the grave, I will redeem them from death."

Hosea 13:24

And thus it behooved Christ to suffer these things, because he had undertaken our cause. And by his precious blood he blotted out our transgressions as a thick cloud from the book of God's remembrance, agreeably to the following text, "I will remove the iniquity of that land in one day."

Zech. 3:9

"Who then shall lay any thing to the charge of God's elect?"

Rom. 8:33

And so from all this what is the sum. The relationship between the man and the woman was designed by God to reflect the eteranl purpose of God in Christ.

Eph. 1.11

Man was created first and had the responsibilty of naming and govering the earth and creatures. Eve was created for a help meet for Adam

Gen. 2.18

Eve was deceived by the serpant and eat the forbiden fruit and gaive it to her husband and he did eat. They both sinned and became guilty before God.

Where Does That Leave Us

Eve became the mother of all living and God made them coats of skin to cover themselves (symbolic of the need and the provision of righteousness that they had in Christ)

The deliverer was promised , the serpant was cursed, multiple sorrow in conception and in childbirth pronounced and the husband was to rule over the wife.

The the church which is described as the body of Christ there are distinctions between the man and the women. They are equal and of equal value before God but we have distict roles. The head of every woman is the man, The elders of churches to be men.

Jesus is our example. The Lord Jesus had a function and role to play. He was coequal with the Farthr and the Spirit and yet he subjected himself to be obedient in all thigs the the Father in order to work out our redemption. In like manner was should seek to fufill our roll and call in our Christain life in marriage , the Church and the world.

Conclusion

I conclude that those who seek to be wiser than what is written in the scripture, as these elders at Warsash, and of the way of salvation and church order, fall into the deception of Satan and work against their declared purpose of functioning as a gospel church. Such pastors are as it was in Jeremiah's day scatter the sheep of Christ and do not gather them at all- to their shame.

When I inform Christian men and women of my conclusions they show that they too have been deceived by saying oh! You have a problem with women. I say no but rather I believe God and the scriptures and am like John the Baptist or more clearly like one of the two witnesses, in Revelation 11 verse 3, who before they were kill spoke clearly in the day of there prophecy. Then the Beast who arose from he bottomless pit slew them.

Observations

It is my observation and suggestion that women have reacted to man's failure to treat them rightly in honouring the weaker vessel and are seek to put a respectable face on feminism. They have turned from the word of God to do this and so are deceived by the devil. The spirit behind this movement is that same spirit which animates the Queen of Heaven and it is not of God.

Repentance is the only hope of recovery to the mind and will of God. The Lord speaks of a bed that these who committed acts of spiritual adultery will be case onto and those who commit such sins with the false prophets Jezebel. I suggest it will be a bed of embarrassment which it will be the Lord doing as he gave them space to repent but did not.

15 APPENDIX 01 COVERING IS AN ISSUE

1 of 2

A new word has come into our religious language. It is "Covering". It is said and believed that every one in Christian ministry needs to be covered if they are to be involved in the work of God. It is said you need to be covered or supported by your church, before you enter into the work of God. Without this it is wrong and you will fail or cannot achieve or do the work of God.

Might I suggest that this is not true and we have no scripture to support this proposition?

A reference to covering does appear in the Corinthian letter stating that a man should not cover his head in the worship of God but the woman should. The suggestion is that when a woman covers her head she signifies she is in subjection to her husband. Paul argues this custom is Christian practice in the churches and is derived from the scriptures of the Old Testament and sights references.

The Head of Every Man

The head of every man is Christ, says the apostle and not the Church.

I maintain we must depend totally upon God for direction. The head of every man is Christ and not an elder, church or religious body of people. I ask one question by whom was Moses, Jonah, John the Baptist, Jesus, or the Apostle Paul covered?

Scripture Deals With Covering

Scripture does actually deal with the issue of covering and its practice and significance. In many religious circles the issue of covering and its scriptural meaning had been lost, ignored or thrown out of the window, only to be replaced by this new expression, "we all need to be covered". In other words the word of God is being ignored or just not seen.

Order In The Godhead, Family & Church

The scripture says the head of every man is Christ, not the church, or its elders. Also in the order of salvation and the revelation of the persons in the trinity the Son subjected himself in humility to the Father in order to work out our salvation. This does not mean Christ is less than or inferior to the Father as this is a covenant relationship of co-equal persons. So it is in the relationship between man and wife. So the head of every woman is her husband, not another man or the church or its elders or a religious organization.

In the case of the women the natural physical head should be veiled or covered in worship to signify she is subject to her man. The covering is an outward sigh of a natural law brought in by God signifying the differences between the man and his wife, which was aggravated by the fall that has come about as the result of the fall of man in the Garden of Eden. The wife is to be subject to her own husband and under him. He is to cover her. This is not chauvinism or sexual discrimination but Christian practice.

Throw Away The Covering

In our modern age women are taking over positions in the church that God designed expressly for men to fulfil.

This modern day phenomenon of throwing away the "covering" which God says a woman should wear, has crept into the religious world and this practice has made an opening for direct disobedience to the word of God. They now do those things the scripture forbids and argue oh that was only a custom of their day and is not a custom of modern days so we ignore the directions.

In the West and in Asia women are appointed elders and pastors and as a result some men have become weak and are unable to stand and contend earnestly for the faith once delivered unto the saints.

The biblical order of Man and women has been lost and is being replaced by this new invention of man- we all need to be covered. This is the new cry.

Covering For All

It is my desire that through this publication I will encourage men to return to the old paths of Christ and His Gospel, and let the bible alone be the only rule of conduct and practice in matters of faith and religion.

Dealing with Offences

This stand will cause offense to many but how we deal with that offence is also spoken of in the scripture. I have shown that when I acted as a Christian and stood for the gospel truth of the Lord Jesus Christ I was opposed by men not directed by scripture. I must not leave the matter with the Lord.

If an offence is committed in any society the scripture teaches the way to deal with the problem. The injured party in a private matter is required to go to that person directly who caused the offence, not to the church, or the elders of the church. They are not to go behind the offender's back but sort it between them both first if possible. Thus the injured party is under Christ and in going directly to that person it opens a way to allow the person to act before the Lord and put an offence right. It allows men the opportunity to exercises grace in the same way God has done to them.

Should this approach fail then an injured party can go with one or two believers seeking to resolve the issue and finally let the problem be known to the church, only if the issue cannot be resolved between them. When Jesus had things against the churches in Revelation they were give the opportunity to repent of face the consequences. It is a fearful thing to fall into the hands of the Living God.

16 APPENDIX 01 COVERING AN ISSUE

2 of 2

History Repeats Its Self

As a member of the Bierton Strict and Particular Baptist Church it was the normal custom for women to cover their heads in worship. Men would pray openly and women remind silent in prayer but they sang hymns. However the customary practice of head covering can take on a different meaning when ones mind is not governed by the spiritual truths of the scripture. This is demonstrated in my book Bierton Strict and Particular Baptists under heading "Hats Or Head Coverings For Ladies", page 212.

Here is the reference.

Hats Or Head Coverings For Ladies

Trouble was on its way in the form of religious oppression. On Sunday morning in 1983 I took to church a friend of mine's daughter. This was the daughter of Dick Holmes who I use to work with as an aerial rigger. She had been through a divorce and was having a difficult time. I suggested she came with me to church, as she needed help from God.

She was dressed in tight black slacks and a short top, which showed all her figure. She had long peroxide blond hair and her face was made up. This mode of dress was a striking contrast to the elderly ladies who dressed very modestly with very little make up on and all ware hats to cover their heads in church.

Unfortunately this was too much for Mrs. Evered who came up to me after the service (I call it a meeting because the meetings of the New Testament churches were not called services) and she said to me the next time I bring a female to chapel I should tell her to wear a hat.

Mrs. Evered said that all Gospel Standard Churches insisted women cover their heads and so should we.

I responded to that by saying, " what ever others do that was their concern they were wrong if they enforced the covering of the head upon a none church member and women visitor having no profession of the Christian faith."

I said she must raise this issue at our church meeting.

This spirit of legalism naturally took me back. Here was a young woman in sever distress needing the mercy and love of God as revealed in Jesus Christ and all Mrs. Evered seemed to be concerned with was the wearing of a Hat.

I knew the principle of a believing women dressing modestly and being in subjection to her own husband and covering her head in worship. I also knew the principle of the woman not exercising authority over the man or teaching a man but this action of Mrs Evered to use the phrase, "took the biscuit".

I was a man and was being instructed by a woman, Mrs Evered, to order or insist a visiting unbelieving female to wear a hat in order to uphold the principle that it was a shame for a woman to worship God without a head covering.

This covering according to the scripture was to show the angels she was in subjection to the man and not usurping authority over him.

Mrs. Evered missed the whole point of the gospel and in her religious zeal to maintaining an outward form of religion transgressed the rule she sought to maintain.

This religious spirit was not of God and I believed the gospel needed to be preached to set men free from such darkness. But who would do this?

Why Cite This Example

The above citation is written to demonstrate and show that the outward religious practice of a head covering can be outwardly correct but for the wrong principle and motive. That does not mean we should disregard the practice and custom.

Man's Head Must Not Be Covered

The head of every man is Christ and so his (physical natural) head must not be covered in the worship of God, this indication is to angels as well as men and he is under Christ's rule directly. The woman is under her husband's rule and so this is signified by her (physical natural) head being covered with a veil or covering.

The Religious World Has Got It Wrong

I have notice that when the wrong view is held and the way of speaking used "every one aught to be covered" then it leads a person to look to an organizing for approval and financial support and not to the Lord. Such people begin to then realize that if they do certain things or act in certain ways then the society with whom they work may disapprove of them and threaten to with draw support.

A man who is under Christ will know the right way to walk and act in any given situation if he is lead by the Spirit of Christ. The moment a man looks to the organization or friends for support he may fall into the trap and try to please man in order to again, acceptance and support. This is the natural man's way and so he cannot walk by faith. The natural man preserves not the things, which are spiritual. The natural man does not depend on God but his own carnal wisdom. The natural man goes against the way of faith.

An example of this error of men looking to man and women taking the lead and getting it wrong can be found in the extract.

Extract From the Daily Diary

Of Trojan Horse International (TULIP) Phils.

Incorporated

December 25th 2002

I went to see Olga Robertson at her home on the reservation of the Bureau of Corrections, at New Bilibid Prison, at Muntinlupa City and had a meal with her friends. Olga had arrived from America and shared with me some of her experiences. She was a women Religious Volunteer (RVO) working in New Bilibid Prison. I gave her a copy of our book, "Trojan Warriors", and she asked me if all these men who had written their testimonies were born again. I stated to her that I was not going to judge them but they must stand by what they have written. I stated that I had not changed a word even though Gordon Smith had wanted me to remove from Hectors Maqueda's testimony his references to TULIP and hard Calvinism, as he called it. He wanted to make the testimony acceptable to all men and not to cause offence. I had to say no to this and maintained we were not to do that as that was changing his testimony. If this happens he wood be like the Pope of Rome seeking to alter things to please men.

Olga told off one of her men helpers who was wearing a hat in her house. She was very curt with him asking what do he think he was doing wearing his hat in her room. I was amused how he obeyed her without question and so I asked Olga did she cover her head when worshipping God. She said NO! And looked at me with a question mark on her face.

The point I was making was that the covering of the head of a man, when in the presence of God in worship, was a dishonour to his head who is the Lord Jesus. This being the Apostle Paul's argument and case.

However Olga Robertson was taking offence at this man wearing a hat in her house and told him so by saying it dishonoured to her by wearing his hat in her dinning room.

The Apostle Paul goes on to say that if a woman did not cover her head in the presence of God in worship then she dishonours her head (the man). Her defiant No told me a lot.

This situation reminded me of Mrs. Evered in "my book The Bierton Crisis".

Contemplations On The Way Of Faith

The spiritual man walks the way of faith, depending upon God and the light of His word and Spirit direct him in every situation. It is the way of faith. Our walk must be by faith. The walk of faith goes against the natural man and way of the carnal nature. We often have to reprove (silently) by doing the right thing, at the right time, regardless of what people think. In such a walk the believer is often alone (but not alone as the Lord it with him).

When men find them selves looking over their shoulders, wondering what will this person of that person think of me, if I do or say or do the approved thing, then that is where Satan has got you. If you find your self not doing things which you know are right before God and proper because you feel others may disapprove of you, then that is Satan ensnaring you so that you will become ineffectual in your work for God. We are told to resist the Devil and he will flee from you.

Forsake The World

It is put as a real proposition that we are called to leave this world, this includes the world of carnal religious people as well, and daily follow Christ. We are required to put away former things, which are not of God, to follow Christ. Our drugs, our laying, our bad ways, to walk with Christ.

The Religious Sinner

The religious sinner must also put away his formal dead religion to follow Christ. We all must take up our Cross and follow Christ. As it would be wrong to encourage a drug dependent   user of drugs or a homosexual to continue his ways. Or for a drinker with drink problems, to remain drinking like a fish.   So in the same way it would be wrong to encourage a religious sinner to continue in his of her idolatry and false religion. They must leave their sinful way, just as a drug dependent and drunkard and sexual deviant, must leave their carnal ways. They must do it today.

We all are all required to walk by faith. Religious sinners exist as well as irreligious sinners exits. All need to be saved from them selves and forsake their world to follow Christ.

David Clarke

Written at Coin, Near Savilla. On a Trojan Horse mission to Spain. 4th May Saturday. Amended. Philippines 5th December 2002 and 1st January 2003.

17 APPENDIX 02 AN ASSIGNMENT FOR THE TEACHERS

Women Elders

The problem of women elders and pastora's as they are called in the Philippines is high lighted in the follow history.

This story is told in my book Before The Cock Crows, in which I tell our my experience working as a missionary to the jails in the Philippines. My brother Michael and I had worked with converted inmate within New Bilibid prison form a Teacher Training College in order to equip qualified men to teach and preach the gospel on their release from prison in their own towns cites and villages. An Assignment for our teacher's at the New Bilibid Teacher Training College was set out as follows.

New Bilibid, (Maximum) Prison Teacher Training College

Essay Assignment

 This assignment question has been put to our teachers and trainers in New Bilibid Prison as these teach the gospel to hundred of inmates in the

"The Big House". New Bilibid Prison houses over 23,500 inmates in three compounds, Minimum, Medium and Maximum Compounds. There are over 1300 men on "Death row" awaiting death by lethal injection. Twenty-two of these men are our "Trojan Warriors".

Our "Trojan Warriors" are preparing to take the gospel to the rest of the prisons in the Philippines (All 1506 district and city jails). Our first man, who has been set apart and was set aside to go to his own city in Baguio to preach the gospel on release from prison in August 2002 is pastor William C. Poloc. His will work closely with our President Rev. Lucas P. Dungatan in the ministry taking the Gospel to prisons in the Philippines in order to, "Set the captives free". His testimony is number 62 in our book Trojan Warriors.

The reason for the question was because both my brother and I had been converted from crime to Christ, we were both were former criminals and had experience the salvation, which comes through Jesus Christ, by believing all what the scripture had written about him and his gospel. We both felt these inmates, some notorious criminals, had now the opportunity not only to learn themselves from the scriptures themselves first hand, and now just like Michael and I had done would be able to pass on their learning, without the influence of the fallen Christian culture in the secular society and what was in the prison.

Assignment Question

Does the Lord Jesus Christ wish women to rule as elders in His Church? Your are required to answer this question in an essay format in 2000 words.

Prelude To The Question and Why

Church history and the world of Christianity is changing. It is believed that the Church should be as a great light to the society in which she lives, to give clear moral guidelines to its people. A Church functioning correctly should help the society rise from poverty and so prosper in every way.

When the Philippines are mentioned to some having a western mind the picture of beautiful women and sunshine comes to mind. It is internationally known and believed by some people that a Philippine wife is the desire of a Western man. This because of her cultural up bringing. It is generally believed the Filipino culture has developed in such a way that the women have good attitude towards the man (her husband), which lends itself to a successful marriage.

On the other hand it has been argued that this cultural phenomenon must be changed because it has left the women vulnerable and open to abuse and exploitation. Strict laws have been passed and enforced to prevent marriages between Philippine women and foreign men. It is argued by some that such laws have been found necessary in order to protect their women and society from abuse. The effect is that these laws prevent the natural migration of Philippine women to other countries should they marry a foreigner.

It is known how ever, by some, that it is poverty that has robbed and damaged the Philippine Culture [1]. The argument goes on to maintain that it is the Catholic religion, which is the cause of the problem, as it breads poverty. So if we get rid of the Catholic Religion we get rid of poverty.

It could be and it may be that the Old Catholic views of the man women relationships may have some mileage. It would be a shame to discard every vestige of good, which has been cultivated over many years, even though the Roman Catholic Church may be so wrong in many other issues.

The moral values, which serve to bring stability to marriages and society, have always been those biblical views expressing of correct relationship between the man and women, children and parents and society and the law of the land.

These moral values dictate that the head of Christ is God, Christ is the head of the man and the man is the head of the women. These statements are not exclusive to the Roman Catholic Church but to all Christians who maintain that the bible is the Word of God.

The bible informs us that God designed the marriage relationship, to reflect the eternal relationship between Christ and his Church (Christ and His Bride). Sexual purity, i.e. no sex before marriage, fidelity in marriage, Marriage for life are values held by all Christians.

That the "curse" and thy desire shall be towards thy husband but he shall rule over thee" is in fact the conflict found in every relationship between man and women.

The women, designed by God, under this curse will always seek to rule over her husband- it is natural to her because she is so very different to the make up of a the man. The man also made in the image of God and under the curse will find this conflict mysterious at times and very hard. He must learn to rule over her, in love, otherwise the marriage will be far from harmonious not being as God so lovingly designed marriage to be. In a successful marriage the scripture will be fulfilled, which expresses the effects of gospel truth, ' In that day the wolf will lay down with the lamb". Guess whom the wolf and lamb may represent.

The position and role of the women, in the sociality of the Church, is also expressed in the bible and the church should reflex this moral and working principle to the world as a great light in this current generation- as an example. The church should not follow a fallen world but be its leader.

This essay should argue that a departure from the bible format which defines clearly the roles and moral codes for church and family life is a sure fore runner of sorrow to our children and children's children.

This is why Jesus admits no divorce (except in the case of adultery and that is not a must) because he wishes the Man to be as he. He will never put his wife away. He redeemed his bride, gave his life for her to cover all her wayward ways. This he did demonstrating his love to her in actions. Under the Law of Moses they had not this light and had hardness of heart- we have the Love of Christ to constrain us)

She in return responds naturally (only through and due to His redeeming grace) willing says "I do- I will love honour and obey you.

Out side this rule of Christ a marriage cannot be as God designed it to be. In marriage children are to learn those necessary things for the make up of good society and its laws. Children need both parents to raise them up. Those children raised in dysfunctional families (due to unresolved conflicts between separated parents) suffer. Then children suffer, Society suffers in fact we will all suffer and have to live with the consequences of our actions.

It is maintained by some that a women ruling as an Elder in a Church is contrary to the will and wish of our Lord Jesus Christ and runs against the grain of scripture. Just like fornication. Homo- sexuality and lesbian relationships run against the grain of the image of God invested in man from the beginning.

Others maintain that the curse in the Garden of Eden has been broken and we now have a new order for Men and Women, as they are equal and can rule as Elders in the Church. That is provided they have the gifts and qualifications to so rule.

The purpose of this essay is to prepare our Trojan Warriors, for the world out side New Bilibid Prison.

In the world you have already found tribulation but in the church, as you will find when you leave prison, you will find great trouble over this issue. Be however of good cheer our Lord Jesus has over come the world. And be thankful He is head of His Church.

David Clarke
Director of Trojan Horse International CM
7th April 2002.
[1] The Philippines Damaged Culture? Earl K. Wilkinson 2001.
A Reflection
Sadly to say the men did not carry out the assignment and Rev. Lucas

Dangatan wrote asking me not to mention anything about the role of women elders etc. in our book "Trojan Warriors" as he did not wish to offend lady pastors and elders who were religious volunteers in the prison and on whom they relied for their financial support. Otherwise they might buy the book. They had many Pastora's (Women Pastors-Elders) and religious volunteers (RVO's) working in New Bilibid Prison. It was a shame that the love of money and the fear of men (women) spoiled their view of Christian true and I was this fact that proved their hearts desire and which I write about in, "Before the Cock Crows", and my new book, "Mission To The Philippines", and now in this book , May, Mary Quite Contrary or alternatively Does The Lord Jesus Want Women to Rule As Elders In His Church ?

My Comments

The revealed teaching, in the Old and New Testament scriptures, concerning the person of the Lord Jesus, are expressed in many Christian Articles of Religion, such at those of Trojan Horse International (TULIP) Phils. Incorporated. A correct understanding in these matters will enable the reader to be free from the errors which this book seeks to deliver the reader from. These articles may be seen in the Appendix 04

The Gospels Teach And Express.

1 The incarnation of Christ i.e. the person of the Son of God becoming man, that which he was not becoming a real man, was of the seed of the woman, the son of David and son of Mary. He was without sin and truly man. He is a divine person uniting the divine and human natures in one complex person Jesus Christ, the God Man. He tabernacled amongst us.

2 The purpose of God, in the creation of the spiritual and material worlds was to manifest his glory to rational creatures capable of appreciating that revelation. The reason for creation was to manifest the Glory of God, not only as the creator and sustainer of the whole universe but the greater glory of God as a display of all the divine perfections and redemption of his people.

This purpose is brought about by predestination.

The gospel of Christ is a revelation of the three divine persons in all their woks and clearly show all the attributes of Gods that are displayed in the redemption that is in Christ.

3 For Jesus Christ came into the world to save his people from their sins. They experience the love, mercy and grace of God in the forgiveness of sins, and are able to behold in wonderment, the wisdom of God, made know to them through their salvation.

4 That the believer, being born again, becomes the true temple of God

and with others are built for an habitation of God through the Spirit.

5 That the Church is the body of Christ, the ground and pillar of the truth, a temple that God has built and not man.

6 That the Son of God, in our nature was the sin offering and the High Priest that was to come.

7 He offered himself , his body and blood, once and for all, in a sacrifice, which can never be repeated. That this sacrifice was that which God taught Adam in the garden of Eden, when He made them coats of skin to cover their shame.

8 His Deity of Jesus was that which sanctified the Gift.

9 There is now no sacrificing priesthood after the order of Aaron.

10 A woman and any other man were disqualified from the priesthood under the law of Moses as declared by the Lord himself.

10 The order of worship and the relationships between man, women, children and society in the Christian church, are taught by the Apostles of Christ. And the Apostles teach that the head of Christ is God, the head of the woman is the man and the women should subject her self to her own husband and must cover her head in worship signifying her subjection to her husband. That the women must remain silent in the church and not teach or usurp authority over the man. That this order is a reminder of the fall of the human race, that took place in the Garden of Eden and of the promise God made concerning the way of redemption through the seed of the women.

11 The Law is fulfilled in Christ and that through the salvation which comes by Jesus Christ all believers enter into the true Sabbath rest that the Sabbath under Moses pointed too.

12 We now have a priesthood of all believers making spiritual sacrifices acceptable to God, by the Mediation of Christ alone and there are no holy places temples of geographic places of worship. And the New Testament order for Christian worship has been prescribed by the Apostles, from which we must not deviate,

Conclusion

It is written Galatians 4 verse 30, "Cast out the bond women and her son for the son of the bond woman shall not be heir with the son of the free women"

And so we should not presume to be wiser than what is written and that obedience to God, in all things, is better than sacrifice. Also every child of God will be proved or tried by the Lord, in just the same way as Abraham was, which is a proving of ones faith. That a tried faith is far more precious

72

that that of silver and gold. So "Cast out the women elders, false Prophetess, Jezebel and her brood, otherwise you too will be cast into a bed. Remember her children will be killed by the Lord".

18 APPENDIX 04 ARTICLES OF RELIGION

Trojan Horse International (TULIP) Phils.

Incorporated

We maintain;

That the scriptures of the Old and New Testaments are given by inspiration of God and are the only rule of faith and practice and that these scriptures reveal the one true and only God who is self existent, infinite and eternal. That there are three self existent co-eternal persons in the Godhead namely the Father the Son and the Holy Ghost and these three are one God and that the Lord Jesus Christ is very God and very man in one glorious complex person.

That God is the creator of both spiritual and material worlds.

That the eternal purpose of God in Christ is to manifest his glory.

That Before the world began God did elect a certain number of the human race unto everlasting life and salvation whom He did predestine to the adoption of Children by Jesus Christ of his own free grace and according to the good pleasure of His will.

That God created the first man Adam upright and all his posterity fell in him. Adam was responsible for the fall of humanity.

The effect of the fall left mankind ruined; this included his mind will and affections. Both Adam and his wife Eve were affected in different ways.

That the Lord Jesus Christ in the fullness of time became incarnate and that he really suffered and died as the substitute for his people (the whole world a term used in scripture, expressing both Jew and Gentile). He made all the satisfaction for their sins, which the law and justice of God could require as well as made a way for the bestowments of all those blessings, which are needful for them for time and eternity.

That the justification of Gods elect is only by the righteousness of Christ imputed to them and received by faith without consideration of any works of righteousness done by them and that the full and free pardon of all there sins and transgressions is only through the full free pardon of all their sins and transgressions is only through the blood of Christ according to the riches of Gods grace.

That the eternal redemption which Christ hath obtained by the shedding of his blood is special and particular that it is only and intentionally designed for the elect of God who only can share its spiritual blessings.

That regeneration, conversion, sanctification and faith are the work of the Almighty efficacious and invincible grace of God the Holy Ghost.

That all those chosen by the Father, redeemed by the Son and sanctified by the Spirit shall certainly and finally persevere unto eternal life.

That the Church is the design of God and is His delight and the Lord, "loves the gates of Zion more than all the dwellings of Jacob".

That baptism of believers by immersion and the Lords Supper are ordinances of Christ.

That marriage was ordained of God to reflect the relationship between Christ and his Church.

There is order in the family, society and Church. The head of every man is Christ, the Head of Christ is God (Father) and the head of every woman is the man. Children are to be subject to their parents and wife's to their own husbands. Society and Church to be subject to magistrates so long this subjection does not oppose the rule of Christ.

Note from the Director

May I suggest that articles of religion are not put up to cause division or controversy but rather use them to prompt the truth as it is in the Lord Jesus Christ? It is unreasonable to expect all people to see and agree on things all at once. Let every one be prepared to learn. A fuller and detailed version of suitable articles of religion my be read in the First London Confession of Particular Baptist in 1644, 2nd edition.

David Clarke (extracted from Trojan Warriors).

19 APPENDIX 05 DR JOHN GILL CORINTHIANS
I Corinthians 11
(Theologian) (1697–1771), English Baptist minister and Calvinist theologian
1 Corinthians 11:1
Be ye followers of me, even as I also am of Christ.

&c] These words more properly close the preceding chapter, than begin a new one, and refer to the rules therein laid down, and which the apostle would have the Corinthians follow him in, as he did Christ: that as he sought, both in private and public, and more especially in his ministerial service, to do all things to the glory of God, and not for his own popular applause, in which he imitated Christ, who sought not his own glory, but the glory of him that sent him; so he would have them do all they did in the name of Christ, and to the glory of God by him: and that as he studied to exercise a conscience void of offence to God and man, in doing which he was a follower of Christ, who was holy in his nature, and harmless and inoffensive in his conversation; so he was desirous that they should likewise be blameless, harmless, and without offence until the day of Christ: and that whereas he endeavoured to please men in all things lawful and indifferent, wherein he copied after Christ, who by his affable and courteous behaviour, and humble deportment, sought to please and gratify all with whom he conversed; so he would have them not to mind high things, but condescend to men of low estates, and become all things to all, that they might gain some as he did: and once more, that as he sought not his own pleasure and advantage, but the salvation of others, in imitation of Christ, who pleased not himself, but took upon him, and bore cheerfully, the reproaches of men, that he might procure good for them; so the apostle suggests, that it would be right in them not to seek to have their own wills in every thing, but rather to please their neighbour for good to edification.

1 Corinthians 11:2

Now I praise you, brethren

The apostle prefaces what he had to say by way of commendation of them; though some think that this is said in an ironical way, because there are many things both in this chapter, and in the following part of this epistle, delivered in a way of reproof; but whoever considers the change of style in (1 Corinthians 11:17) will easily see, that this must be spoken seriously here, and is designed to raise the attention to what he was about to say, and to prepare their minds to receive, and take in good part, what he should say by way of rebuke; who could not well be angry when he praised them for what was praiseworthy in them, and reproved them for that which was blameable. The things he commends them for are as follow,

That ye remember me in all things;

that is, either that they were mindful of him, though at a distance from them, and had such a veneration for him, and paid such respect to him, and to his judgment, as to write to him to have his sense about any point of doctrine, or case of conscience which had any difficulty in them; or that they bore in memory the doctrines of the Gospel which he had delivered among them; see (1 Corinthians 15:2) The Arabic version reads, "that ye remember my sayings and deeds"; the doctrines he preached among them, and the examples he set them:

and keep the ordinances, as I delivered them to you;

meaning, among the rest, if not principally, baptism and the Lord's supper, which he received from Christ, and delivered unto them; see (1 Corinthians 11:23) and which they, at least many of them, kept and observed in the faith of Christ, from a principle of love to him, and with a view to his glory, and that as to the form and manner in which they were delivered to them by the apostle, agreeably to the mind of Christ; but was the apostle alive now, would, or could he praise the generality of those that are called Christians on this account? No; neither of these ordinances in common are kept as they were delivered: as to baptism, it is not attended to either as to subject or mode, both are altered, and are different from the original institution; and the Lord's supper is prostituted to the vilest of men; and, what is "monstrum horrendum", is made a test and qualification for employment in civil and military offices under the government.

1 Corinthians 11:3

But I would have you to know

Though they were mindful of him, and retained in memory many things he had declared among them, and kept the ordinances as delivered to them; yet there were some things in which they were either ignorant, or at least did not so well advert to, and needed to be put in mind of, and better informed about: and as the apostle was very communicative of his knowledge in every point, he fails not to acquaint them with whatsoever might be instructive to their faith, and a direction to their practice:

That The Head Of Every Man Is Christ

Christ is the head of every individual human nature, as he is the Creator and Preserver of all men, and the donor of all the gifts of nature to them; of the light of nature, of reason, and of all the rational powers and faculties; he is the head of nature to all men, as he is of grace to his own people: and so he is as the Governor of all the nations of the earth, who whether they will or no are subject to him; and one day every knee shall bow to him, and every tongue confess that he is the Lord of all. Moreover, Christ is the head of every believing man; he is generally said to be the head of the church, and so of every man that is a member of it: he is a common public head, a representative one to all his elect; so he was in election, and in the covenant of grace; so he was in time, in his death, burial, resurrection, and ascension to, and entrance into heaven; and so he is now as an advocate and intercessor there: he is the political head of his people, or an head in such sense, as a king is the head of his nation: he is also an economical head, or in such sense an head as an husband is the head of his wife, and as a parent is the head of his family, and as a master is the head of his servants; for all these relations Christ sustains: yea, he is a natural head, or is that to his church, as an human head is to an human body: he is a true and proper head, is of the same nature with his body, is in union to it, communicates life to it, is superior to it, and more excellent than it. He is a perfect head, nothing is wanting in him; he knows all his people, and is sensible of their wants, and does supply them; his eye of love is always on them; his ears are open to their cries; he has a tongue to speak to them, and for them, which he uses; and he smells a sweet savour in them, in their graces and garments, though they are all his own, and perfumed by himself: there are no vicious humours in this head, flowing from thence to the body to its detriment, as from Adam to his posterity, whose head he was; but in Christ is no sin, nothing but grace, righteousness, and holiness, spring from him. There's no deformity nor deficiency in him; all fullness of grace dwells in him to supply the members of his body; he is an one, and only head, and an ever living and everlasting one.

And the head of the woman is the man,

The man is first in order in being, was first formed, and the woman out of him, who was made for him, and not he for the woman, and therefore must be head and chief; as he is also with respect to his superior gifts and excellencies, as strength of body, and endowments of mind, whence the woman is called the weaker vessel; likewise with regard to pre-eminence or government, the man is the head; and as Christ is the head of the church, and the church is subject to him, so the husband is the head of the wife, and she is to be subject to him in everything natural, civil, and religious. Moreover, the man is the head of the woman to provide and care for her, to nourish and cherish her, and to protect and defend her against all insults and injuries.

And The Head Of Christ Is God

That is, the Father, not as to his divine nature, for in respect to that they are one: Christ, as God, is equal to his Father, and is possessed of the same divine perfections with him; nor is his Father the head of him, in that sense; but as to his human nature, which he formed, prepared, anointed, upheld, and glorified; and in which nature Christ exercised grace on him, he hoped in him, he believed and trusted in him, and loved him, and yielded obedience to him; he always did the things that pleased him in life; he prayed to him; he was obedient to him, even unto death, and committed his soul or spirit into his hands: and all this he did as to his superior, considered in the human nature, and also in his office capacity as Mediator, who as such was his servant; and whose service he diligently and faithfully performed, and had the character from him of a righteous one; so that God is the head of Christ, as he is man and Mediator, and as such only.

1 Corinthians 11.4

Every man praying or prophesying

This is to be understood of praying and prophesying in public, and not in private; and not to be restrained to the person that is the mouth of the congregation to God in prayer, or who preaches to the people in the name of God; but to be applied to every individual person that attends public worship, that joins in prayer with the minister, and hears the word preached by him, which is meant by prophesying; for not foretelling future events is here meant, but explaining the word of God, the prophecies of the Old Testament, or any part of Scripture, unless singing of psalms should rather be designed, since that is sometimes expressed by prophesying: so in

1 Samuel 10.5

"thou shalt meet a company of prophets coming down from the high place, with a psaltery, and a tabret, and a pipe, and a harp before them, and they shall prophesy". The Targum renders it thus, "and they shall sing praise"; upon which Kimchi observes, that it is as if it was said, their prophecy shall be, "songs" and praises to God, spoken by the Holy Ghost. So in

1 Samuel 19.23, 1 Samuel 19.24

It is said of Saul, that he "went on and prophesied". The Targum is, he went on, "and praised". And again, "he stripped off his clothes also, and prophesied". Targum, "and praised", or sung praise. Once more, in

1 Chronicles 25.1-3

it is said of Asaph, and others, that they "should prophesy with harps, with psalteries, and with cymbals"; which Kimchi explains of Asaph's singing vocally, and of his sons playing upon musical instruments.

Having his head covered;

which, it seems, was the custom of some of them so to do in attendance on public worship. This they either did in imitation of the Heathens, who worshipped their deities with their heads covered, excepting Saturn and Hercules, whose solemnities were celebrated with heads unveiled, contrary to the prevailing customs and usages in the worship of others; or rather in imitation of the Jews, who used to veil themselves in public worship, through a spirit of bondage unto fear, under which they were, and do to this day; and with whom it is a rule, that

"a man might not stand and pray, neither with his girdle on, nor with his head uncovered; nor with his feet uncovered."

Accordingly it is said of Nicodemus ben Gorion,

"that he went into the school grieved, and "veiled himself", and stood in prayer;"and a little after that

"that he went into the sanctuary and "veiled" himself, and stood and prayed;" though the Targum on

Judges 5.2

suggests,``that the wise men sit in the synagogues, "with the head uncovered", to teach the people the words of the law;" and on

Judges 5.9

has these words,

"Deborah in prophecy said, I am sent to praise the Scribes of Israel, who when they were in tribulation did not cease from expounding the law; and so it was beautiful for them to sit in the synagogues, "with the head uncovered", and teach the people the words of the law, and bless and confess before the Lord;" but it seems that a different custom had now prevailed; now from this Gentile or judaizing practice, the apostle would dissuade them by observing, that such an one that uses it, "dishonoureth his head"; meaning either in a figurative, spiritual, and mystical sense, his head Christ, in token of the liberty received from him, and because he is above in heaven, and clear of all sin, the head must be uncovered in public worship; or otherwise the reverse is suggested of him, which is highly to dishonour him, and is the sense many interpreters give into. Rather the reason should be, because Christ, the believer's head, appears for him in heaven, opens a way of access for him, gives him audience and acceptance in his person, and through his blood and righteousness; and therefore should appear with open face and head uncovered, as a token of freedom and boldness; otherwise he dishonours his head as if his blood and sacrifice were not effectual, and his intercession not prevalent. But the natural head, taken in a literal sense, is rather meant; and the sense is, that by covering it, it looks as if he was guilty and ashamed, and in subjection; whereas to appear uncovered expresses freedom, boldness, and superiority, like himself, who is the head of the woman; whereas to be covered, as with a woman's veil or hood, is effeminate, unmanly, and dishonourable.

20 DR JOHN GILL 1 CORINTHIANS 11 5

1 Corinthians 11.5

But every woman that prayeth or prophesieth

Not that a woman was allowed to pray publicly in the congregation, and much less to preach or explain the word, for these things were not permitted them: see

1 Corinthians 14.34, 1 Corinthians 14.35 , 1 Timothy 2.12,

But it designs any woman that joins in public worship with the minister in prayer, and attends on the hearing of the word preached, or sings the praises of God with the congregation, as we have seen, the word prophesying signifies,

with her head uncovered.

It may seem strange from whom the Corinthian women should take up this custom, since the Jewish women were not allowed to go into the streets, or into any open and public place, unveiled[2] . It was a Jewish law, that they should go out no where bare headed [3] yea, it was reckoned scandalous and ignominious to do so. Hence it is said,[4] , "that uncovering of the head is a reproach" to the daughters of Israel: and concerning the adulterous woman, it is represented as said by the priest [5],

"thou hast separated from the way of the daughters of Israel; for the way or custom of the daughters of Israel is "to have their heads covered"; but thou hast gone "in the ways of the Gentiles", who walk with head bare."

So that their it should seem that these Corinthians followed the examples of the Heathens: but then, though it might be the custom of some nations for women to go abroad bare headed; yet at their solemnities, where and when they were admitted, for they were not everywhere and always, they used to attend with their heads veiled and covered[6]. Mr. Mede takes notice indeed of some Heathen priestesses, who used to perform their religious rites and sacrifices with open face, and their hair hanging down, and locks spreading, in imitation of whom these women at Corinth are thought to act. However, whoever behaved in this uncomely manner, whose example soever she followed, the apostle says,

dishonoureth her head;

not her husband, who is her head in a figurative sense, and is dishonoured by her not being covered; as if she was not subject to him, or because more beautiful than he, and therefore shows herself; but her natural head, as appears from the reason given:

for that is even all one as if she were shaven;

to be without a veil, or some sort of covering on her head, according to the custom of the country, is the same thing as if her head was shaved; and everyone knows how dishonourable and scandalous it is for a woman to have her head shaved; and if this is the same, then it is dishonourable and scandalous to her to be without covering in public worship. And this shows, that the natural head of the man is meant in the preceding verse, since the natural head of the woman is meant in this.

---

2   Maimon. Hilch. Ishot, c. 24. sect. 12.

3 T. Bab. Cetubot, fol. 72. 1.

4 R. Sol. Jarchi in Numb. v. 19.

5   Bemidbar Rabba, sect. 9. fol. 193. 2.

6   Alex. ab Alex. Genial. Dier. l. 4. c. 17.

1 Corinthians 11.6

For if the woman be not covered

That is, if her head is not covered with some sort of covering, as is the custom of the place where she lives,

let her also be shorn;

let her hair be cut short; let her wear it as men do theirs; and let her see how she will look, and how she will like that, and how she will be looked upon, and liked by others; everybody will laugh at her, and she will be ashamed of herself: but if it be a shame for a woman to be shorn or shaven: as it is accounted in all civilized nations: the very Heathens[7] speak of it as a thing abominable, and of which there should not be one single dreadful example: then let her be covered; with a veil, or any sort of covering in common use.

1 Corinthians 11.7

For a man indeed ought not to cover his head

The Ethiopic version adds, "whilst he prays"; which is a proper interpretation of the words, though a wrong version; for the apostle's meaning is not, that a man should not have his head covered at any time, but whilst he is in public worship, praying, prophesying, or singing of psalms: the reason is,

Forasmuch as he is the image and glory of God.

The apostle speaks of man here as in his first creation, in his state of innocence before his fall; but now he has sinned and defaced this image, and come short of this glory; which lay partly in his body being made after the exemplar of the body of Christ, the idea of which God had in his eternal mind, and according to which he shaped the body of Adam: and partly in his soul, in that righteousness and holiness, wisdom and knowledge, and all other excellent gifts in which it was formed. So the Jews[8] say, the understanding is "the glory of God". And it chiefly lay in the power and dominion he had over all the creatures, and even over the woman when made; at least this is principally respected here, in which there is such a shine and representation of the glory and majesty, power and dominion of God; and therefore man ought to worship him with his head uncovered, where this image and glory of God is most illustriously displayed: not but that the woman, is the image and glory of God also, and was made as man, after his image and likeness, with respect to internal qualities, as righteousness, holiness, knowledge and with regard to her power over the other creatures, though in subjection to man; but yet man was first originally and immediately the image and glory

---

7 Vid. Apul. Metamorph. l. 2. p. 21.

8   Maimon. in Misn. Chagiga, c. 2. sect 1. 1.

of God, the woman only secondarily and mediately through man. The man is more perfectly and conspicuously the image and glory of God, on account of his more extensive dominion and authority:

but the woman is the glory of the man;

being made out of him, and for his help and assistance, and to be a crown of honour and glory to him. The apostle speaks the sense, and in the language of the Jews. The words in

Isaiah 44.13

"After the figure of a man, according to the beauty of a man", are by the Targum rendered, "after the likeness of a man, after the glory of a woman"; and the note of a famous interpreter of theirs upon the last clause is, "this is the woman", "who is the glory of her husband"; but why is she to be covered for this reason, when the man is to be uncovered? It is to be observed, that it is in the presence and worship of God that the one is to be uncovered, and the other covered; the one being the glory of God, and therefore to be uncovered before him; and the other the glory of man, and therefore to be covered before God; and especially, since being first in the transgression, she who is man's glory has been the means of his shame and disgrace. The Jews seem to make this the reason of the difference; they ask[9], "why does a man go out with his head uncovered, and a woman with her head covered? It is answered, it is like to one that has committed a sin, and he is ashamed of the children of men, therefore she goes , "with her head covered"."

1 Corinthians 11.8

For the man is not of the woman

In the present state of things, and according to the ordinary course of generation and propagation of mankind, man is of the woman, though not without the means of man; he is conceived in her, bore by her, and born of her; but the apostle respects the original formation of man, as he was immediately made by God out of the dust of the earth, before the woman was in being, and so not of her:

but the woman of the man;

she was made out of his rib, and took both her name and nature from him; God was the author, and man the matter of her being; her original under God, is owing to him; and therefore as he was first in being, he must be superior to her: this serves to prove all that has been as yet said; as that man is the head of the woman, the woman is the glory of man, what he may glory in as being from him; and therefore there should be this difference in their appearance at public worship.

---

9   Bereshit Rabba, sect. 17. fol. 15. 1.

1 Corinthians 11:9

Neither was the man created for the woman

To be subservient to her; for she was not in being when he was created; and though it is the proper business of man to provide for, take care of, and defend the woman, as the weaker vessel, yet these were not the original ends of his creation; he was made for God, for his service and glory:

but the woman for the man;

to be an help meet for him, who was already created; to be a companion and associate of his, both in religious worship and in civil life; and for the procreation and education of children.

21 DR JOHN GILL 1 CORINTHIANS

1 Corinthians 11:10

For this cause ought the woman to have power on her head,

&c. The generality of interpreters, by power, understand the veil, or covering on the woman's head, as a sign of the man's power over her, and her subjection to him; which Dr. Hammond endeavours to confirm, by observing that the Hebrew word (dydr) , which signifies a woman's veil, or hood, comes from a root which signifies power and dominion; but in that he is mistaken, for the word is derived not from to rule, govern, or exercise power and authority, but from, to expand, stretch out, or draw over, as a woman's veil is drawn over her head and face. The Greek word ($\varepsilon\xi$ουσια) more properly signifies the power she had of putting on and off her covering as she pleased, according as times, places, and persons; made it necessary:

Because of the angels;

various are the senses given of these words, some taking them in a proper, others in a figurative sense: some in a proper sense of angels, and these either good or bad. Tertullian[10] understands them of evil angels, and that a woman should cover her head in time of worship, lest they should lust after her; though much rather the reason should be, lest they should irritate and provoke lust in others: but it is better to understand them of good angels, who attend the assemblies of the saints, and observe the air and behaviour of the worshippers; wherefore women should cover their heads with respect to them, and not give offence to those pure spirits, by an indecent appearance: it is agreeable to the notions of the Jews, that angels attend public prayers, and at the expounding of the word; they often speak[11] of an angel, (twlpth le hnwmmh) "that is appointed over prayers"; hence[12]

---

10 De Veland. Virg. c. 7.

11 Shemot Rabba, sect. 21. fol. 106. 2. Zohar. in Gen. fol. 97. 2.

12 De Oratione, c. 15.

Tertullian seems to have took his notion of an angel of prayer: and of angels being present at expounding of the Scriptures, take the following story F8; ``it happened to Rabban Jochanan ben Zaccai, that he was riding upon an ass, and as he was journeying, R. Eleazar ben Arach was leading an ass after him; he said to him, Rabbi, teach me one chapter in the work of Mercavah (Ezekiel's vision); he replied to him, not so have I taught you, nor in the Mercavah a single man, unless he was a wise man by his own industry; he answered him, Rabbi, give me leave to say one thing before thee, which thou hast taught me; immediately Rabban Jochanan ben Zaccai alighted from his ass and "veiled himself", and sat upon a stone under an olive tree; he said to him, Rabbi, why dost thou alight off from the ass? he replied, is it possible that thou shouldst expound in the work of Mercavah, and the Shekinah be with us, "and the ministering angels join us", and I ride upon an ass?"

And a little after, "R. Joshua and R. Jose the priest were walking on the road, they said, yea, let us expound in the work of Mercavah; R. Joshua opened and expounded, and that day was the solstice of Tammuz, and the heavens were thickened with clouds, and there appeared the form of a bow in the cloud, "and the ministering angels gathered together", "and came to hear": as the children of men gather together, and come to see the rejoicings of the bridegroom and bride."

Moreover, this veiling of the woman in public worship because of angels, may be an imitation of the good angels, who when they sung the praises of God, and adored and glorified his perfections, covered their faces and their feet with their wings,

Isaiah 6:1-3

Many understanding these words in a figurative sense, and in this also they are not agreed; some by angels think young men are meant, who, for their gracefulness and comeliness, are compared to angels; others good men in general, that attend religious worship; others ministers of the word, called angels often in the book of the Revelations; which last seems to be most agreeable of any of these senses; and the women were to cover their heads, that they might not offend either of these, or stir up any impure desires in them; see

Ecclesiastes 5:6

but as these words follow the account given of the creation of the woman from the man, and for his sake; this may have no reference to her conduct in public worship, but to the power she had of using her covering, or taking it off, or putting it on, at the time of her espousals to a man; which was sometimes done by proxy, or messengers, whom the Jews call , "angels"[13]; their canon is, ``a man may espouse (a wife) by himself, "or by his angel", or messenger; and a woman may be espoused by herself, or by her angel, or messenger:" wherefore because of these angels, or messengers, that came to espouse her to such, she had power over her head to take off her veil, and show herself, if she thought fit; or to keep it on, as expressing her modesty; or just as she pleased, when she by them was espoused to a man, for whose sake she was made; which sense, after Dr. Lightfoot, many learned men have given into, and seems probable.

1 Corinthians 11:11

Nevertheless, neither is the man without the woman

This is said, partly to repress the pride and insolence of man, that he might not be too much elated with himself, and his superiority over the woman, and look with any degree of disdain and contempt upon her, and treat her with indifference and neglect; and partly to comfort the woman, that she might not be dejected with the condition and circumstances in which she was, since the one is not without the other; nor can they be so truly comfortable and happy, as not the man without the woman, who was made for an help meet for him,

so neither the woman without the man in the Lord.

The phrase "in the Lord" is added, to show that it is the will of God, and according to his ordination and appointment, that the one should not be without the other; or it may design that lawful conjunction and copulation, of one man and one woman together, according to the will of the Lord, which distinguishes it from all other impure mixtures and copulations. The Arabic version reads it, "in the religion of the Lord"; and the sense is, that the one is not without the other in religious worship, and in the enjoyment of religious privileges; that though the woman may not pray publicly and expound the Scriptures, yet she may join in prayer, and hear the word preached, sing the praises of God, and enjoy all ordinances; for in Christ no distinction of sex is regarded, men and women are all one in him, and equally regenerated, justified, and pardoned, and will be glorified together.

1 Corinthians 11:12

For as the woman is of the man

Originally; so Eve was of Adam, made out of one of his ribs: even so is the man also by the woman;

Now man is born of a woman, he is conceived of one, and brought into the world by one. This is the way in which mankind is propagated, the species

---

13 Misn. Kiddushin, c. 2. sect. 1

preserved, continued, and increased; and therefore there is no reason why the woman should be despised, or the man should be lifted up with himself above her, since they are so dependent upon, and so useful to each other:

but all things of God.

The Arabic version reads it, "all creatures are of God"; which is true, but not the truth of these words, which are to be restrained to the subject of the discourse; as that both the man and the woman are of God; they are made by him, and after his image and likeness; that the man is the glory of God, and the woman the glory of the man; the authority of the man over the woman, and the subjection of the woman to the man, are of God, and according to his constitution and appointment; as also that the woman should be of the man, and for his sake, and that the man should be by the woman, and neither should be without the other: these are not things of human constitution, but are settled by the wise counsel of God, and therefore to be cheerfully submitted to, as the best order of things.

1 Corinthians 11:13

Judge in yourselves

The apostle having gone through a variety of reasoning and arguments, showing the superiority of the man to the woman, by which he would prove, that the one should be covered, and the other uncovered, returns to his subject again, and appeals to the common sense and understanding of the Corinthians, and makes them themselves judges of the matter; suggesting that the thing was so clear, and he so certain of what he had advanced being right, that he leaves it with them, not doubting but that they would, upon a little reflection within themselves, join with him in this point:

is it comely that a woman pray unto God uncovered?

in you judgment you can never think so, however pleasing and gratifying such a sight may be, to the lust of the flesh, and to the lust of the eye; he does not mention prophesying, only instances in praying; but it is to be understood of one, as of another; and his meaning is, that it is an uncomely thing in a woman to appear in public service with her head uncovered, whether it be in joining in the public prayers, or in singing of psalms, or in hearing the word expounded; and though the apostle does not put the case of the man's praying to God, or prophesying in his name with his head covered, yet his sense is the same of that, as of the woman's.

1 Corinthians 11:14

Doth not even nature itself teach you

By nature is either meant, the law and light of nature, reason in man, common sense, or rather custom, which is second nature; and which, in this case, must be restrained to the Greeks and Jews; for though among the Grecians the men cut their hair, and did not suffer it to grow long, as also did the Jews, yet there were many nations [14] who did not, even at that time, observe such a rule or custom; but as the Jews and Greeks were the persons chiefly, if not solely, known to the Corinthians, the apostle signifies, that the usages of these people might direct and inform them in this matter: that if a man have long hair it is a shame unto him; he looks unmanly and womanish, and exposes himself to ridicule and contempt.

1 Corinthians 11:15

But if a woman have long hair

And wears it, without cutting it, as men do:

it is a glory to her;

it is comely and beautiful; it is agreeable to her sex, she looks like herself; it becomes and adorns her: for her hair is given her for a covering; not instead of a covering for her head, or any other part of her body, so that she needs no other: we read indeed of the daughter of Nicodemus ben Gorion, that she was obliged to make use of her hair for a covering in such a sense[15]; "it happened to R. Jochanan ben Zaccai that he rode upon an ass, and went out of Jerusalem, and his disciples went after him; he saw a young woman gathering barley corns out of the dung of the Arabian cattle; when she saw him, "she covered herself with her hair", and stood before him:" but this covering was made use of, not of choice, but by force, through her poverty, she having no other; this was not the custom of the nation, nor was the hair given to women for a covering in this sense, nor used by them as such, unless by Eve before the fall; but is rather an indication that they want another covering for their head, it not being so decent that their long hair should be seen. The Jewish women used to esteem it an immodest thing for their hair to be seen, and therefore they took care, as much as possible, to hide it under another covering; "one woman, whose name was Kimchith, had seven sons, and they all ministered in the high priesthood; the wise men said unto her, what hast thou done, that thou art so worthy? she replied to them, all my days the beams of my house never saw (yrev yelq) , "the plaits of my hair" [16]; " that is, they were never seen by any person, even within her house.

1 Corinthians 11:16

But if any man seem to be contentious

---

14 Alex. ab. Alex. Genial. Dier. l. 5. c. 18. Servius in Virgil. Aeneid. l. 10. prope finem.

15 T. Bab. Cetubot, fol. 66. 2.

16 T. Bab. Yoma, fol. 47. 1.

That is, if anyone will not be satisfied with reasons given, for men's praying and prophesying with their heads uncovered, and women's praying and prophesying with their heads covered; but will go on to raise objections, and continue carping and cavilling, showing that they contend not for truth, but victory, can they but obtain it any way; for my part, as if the apostle should say, I shall not think it worth my while to continue the dispute any longer; enough has been said to satisfy any wise and good man, anyone that is serious, thoughtful, and modest; and shall only add, we have no such custom, nor the churches of God; meaning, either that men should appear covered, and women uncovered in public service, and which should have some weight with all those that have any regard to churches and their examples; or that men should be indulged in a captious and contentious spirit; a man that is always contending for contention sake, and is continually cavilling and carping at everything that is said and done in churches, and is always quarrelling with one person or another, or on account of one thing or another, and is constantly giving uneasiness, is not fit to be a church member; nor ought he to be suffered to continue in the communion of the church, to the disturbance of the peace of it. This puts me in mind of a passage in the Talmud . "The Rabbans teach, that after the departure of R. Meir, R. Judah said to his disciples, do not let the disciples of R. Meir enter here, (שְׁקִנְתְּרָנִין הֵן מִפְּנֵי) , "because they are contentious".

1 Corinthians 11:17

Now in this that I declare unto you

The Syriac version reads, "this is what I command"; which some refer to what he had been discoursing of, adding to his arguments, and the examples of the church, his own orders and command, that men should worship God publicly, uncovered, and women covered; though it seems rather to respect what follows, what the apostle was about to declare unto them; concerning which he says,

I praise you not;

as he did in (1 Corinthians 11:2) that they were mindful of him, remembered his doctrines, and kept the ordinances in the manner he had delivered them to them: and it should seem by this, that the greater part of them were not to be blamed, though some few were, for their irregular and indecent appearance in public worship, men with a covering on their heads, and women without one; but in what he was about to say, he could not praise them at all:

that you come together;

to the house of God, to pray unto him, to sing his praises, to hear his word, and attend his ordinances, particularly the Lord's supper:

not for the better;

for edification and instruction, for the quickening and comforting of your souls; that you may grow in grace and knowledge, become more holy, zealous, fruitful, and useful:

but for the worse;

to indulge luxury and intemperance, to encourage heresies, schisms, and divisions, and so grow more carnal, scandalous, and useless.

1 Corinthians 11:18

For first of all, when ye come together in the church

The place where the church met together to perform divine service, called "one place". (1 Corinthians 11:20) and is distinguished from their own "houses", (1 Corinthians 11:22) and the first thing he took notice of as worthy of dispraise and reproof, in their religious assemblies, were their animosities and factions:

I hear that there be divisions among you:

schisms and parties, either about their ministers, one being for Paul, another for Apollos, and another for Cephas; or in the celebration of the Lord's supper, and that which went before it, they going into separate bodies, and partook by themselves, and each took his own supper before another, one ate, and another did not. This the apostle had heard from the house of Chloe:

and I partly believe it;

meaning, either that this was the practice of a part of the church to do so, though not of them all; or that part of the report that had been made to him was true; though he hoped in that charity which hopeth all things, that it was not quite so bad as was feared or represented, since things are generally heightened and increased by fame; but yet he had it from such good hands, that he could not but believe there was something in it. So the Syriac version renders it, "and something, something I believe".

22 APPENDIX 06 TESTIMONY OF JOHN BUNYAN

John Bunyan (1628-1688) was an English, Particular Baptist, Puritan author and preacher. He is the author of more than 60 books but most famously known for his classic novel, "The Pilgrim's Progress" Grace abounding to the Chief Of Sinners". Bunyan's writings share the same clear and direct style as his immensely popular sermons, which were known to draw crowds of around 3,000 individuals on Sunday.

In 1683 Bunyan published a tract entitled "A Case of Conscience

Resolved" dealing with women who segregated themselves and were gathering together privately for worship (with no men present). He was asked for his opinion on this practice and to respond to a Mr. Keach who permitted and defended these women's meetings. In his tract John Bunyan expresses disagreement with the practice and lays out a case for why worship must be men and women together, with men taking the lead.

Near the end of this tract John Bunyan refers to 1 Corinthians 11 several times and sheds light on his understanding of head covering.

Here's how he starts:

WOMEN! They are an ornament in the church of God on earth, as the ANGELS are in the church in heaven. Betwixt whom also there is some comparison, for they cover their faces in acts of worship (Isa 6:2; 1 Cor 11:10).

1) Bunyan saw a parallel between the angels in Isaiah 6 and women in worship who both veil themselves in the presence of God.

Continuing on he says:

But as the angels in heaven are not Christ, and so not admitted to the mercy-seat to speak to God, so neither are women on earth, [but] the man; who is to worship with open face before him, and to be the mouth in prayer for the rest. As the angels then cry, Holy, Holy, Holy, with faces covered in heaven: So let the women, cry, Holy, Holy, Holy, with their faces covered on earth: Yea, thus they should do, because of the angels. "For this cause ought the woman to have power," that is a covering, "on her head, because of the angels" (1 Cor 11:10). Not only because the angels are present, but because women and angels, as to their worship, in their respective places, have a semblance. For the angels are inferior to the great man Christ, who is in heaven; and the woman is inferior to the man, that truly worships God in the church on earth.

2) Bunyan continues on with several comparisons between women and angels. Just as angels do not approach the mercy seat to speak to God, women do not speak in church meetings (1 Cor 14:33-35). Just as angels cover their faces in Heaven, women cover on earth. Just as angels are inferior to God, women are inferior to men. He then appeals to 1 Cor 11:10 for support not only because angels are present in worship but also because they are like women.

He continues:

Methinks, holy and beloved sisters, you should be content to wear this power, or badge of your inferiority, since the cause thereof arose at first from yourselves. It was the woman that at first the serpent made use of, and by whom he then overthrew the world: wherefore the women, to the world's end, must wear tokens of her underlingship in all matters of worship.

3) Bunyan exhorted women to cover "in all matters of worship" which he understands as when the church corporately meets together. He said this was to be done "to the world's end" showing that he understood this practice to be ongoing and permanent.

To say nothing of that which she cannot shake off, to wit, her pains and sorrows in child-bearing, which God has riveted to her nature, there is her silence, and shame, and a covering for her face, in token of it, which she ought to be exercised with, whenever the church comes together to worship (Gen 3:16; 1 Tim 2:15; 1 Cor 11:13; 1 Tim 2:9). 6)

Just as the women's pain in child-bearing never ends, so also is she to worship in silence and with a covering forever "whenever the church comes together to worship". Bunyan saw the covering as a "token of her shame" which he connects to Eve's disobedience in Genesis.

Bunyan also referenced head covering when talking about "extraordinary" women in the Bible who prophesied, taught or had authority:

4) Though this I must say concerning them, they ought to, and did, notwithstanding so high a calling, still bear about with them the badge of their inferiority to them that were prophets indeed. And hence it is said, under pain of being guilty of disorder, that if they prayed in the church, or prophesied there, with their head uncovered, they then dishonoured their head (1 Cor 11:5). The prophetesses were below the prophets, and their covering for their heads was to be worn in token thereof...

5) He notes that even though these women had extraordinary function, they still would have worn a covering in church. Finally he says as a good summary of his view:

The men are admitted in such worship, to stand with open face before God, a token of much admittance to liberty and boldness with God, a thing denied to the women (1 Cor 11:4,5).

Summary of John Bunyans views:

The believing woman should cover her head in worship and the man should be uncovered. This is a reminder of the fall and her subjection to he husband.

References

1. John Bunyan – A Case of Conscience Resolved

2. Websters 1828 Dictionary has the following definitions for 'inferior' in addition to lower value 1. Lower in place. 2. Lower in station, age, or rank in life. Pay due respect to those who are superior in station, and due civility

to those who are inferior.

Conclusion

I have described how the controversy regarding women elders arose at the Jesus is Lord Church in Warsash and recorded how I responded to what I believed was a serious error on the part of the elders at the church.

I have expressed why I believe it wrong to appoint a women as an elder in a Christian church basing my views upon what the scriptures teach. I have also pointed out the serious repercussions of some who rejected the word of God, as in the case of King Saul.

I have also pointed out that the relationship between man and woman, in marriage, is designed to reflect that relationship between Christ and his church, a pattern designed by God before the world began.

I have pointed out that Adam and Eve were created in the image of God but Adam to be the first to be created and Eve taken form his side and made as a help meet for him. Adam name all the creatures.

I have pointed to the fact of the fall of Adam and Eve, in the garden of Eden, and how the perpetual reminder of their disobedience is experience by mans toil by the sweet of his brow and the pain women experience in child baring. The reminder also being given through the instruction for the woman to be subject to her own husband.

That is also pointed to when a woman covers her head in worship and man does not covered head and also the fact of the instruction for the woman to remain silent in the church. A marriage should reflect that relationship between Christ and his Church where the man should be a Christ who loved and gave himself for his church and the church being subject to her husband as unto Christ.

My View

I have personally experienced the salvation which in by the Lord Jesus Christ. This transformed my life and brought me out from a criminal life style to that pleasing to God and society. The method and means was through my reading and understanding, as best I could, the plain teaching of the bible. To these truths I point to when telling others of the way of salvation. When any one becomes a Christian they seek and desire to do those things that please the Lord, they are not argumentative but humbled and teachable.

These elders and those who are wiser than what is written in scripture are not to be relied on as they have become blind guides, not know the direction they are going and lead others astray.

Battle of The Sexes

There have been many books and films written on the subject that identify the differences between men and women, such as "My Fair Lady", staring Rex Harrison and Sophie Lorraine

"The Battle of the Sexes", staring Peter Sellers and books like, "Men are from Mars, Women are from Venus" and so on and they are all humorous.

How ever the common tend has become such that if you point out these differences you will be labelled as being Sexist or a Male Chauvinist However it has become common place for women to complain. It seems the modern man and modern women refuse to acknowledge there is a sociological,l physiological and genetic difference between the man and the women simply because they cannot tell the reason for these difference, they simply believe it is a matter of evolution and up bringing.

It is my belief that the bible tells the reason for these differences and how to deal with them. This is why I have written this book. Ignore the book at your peril.

The following is a humours illustration pointing out the differenced between men and women that men of this world have observed

23 APPENDIX 07 THE RULES

The FEMALE always makes The Rules.

The Rules are subject to change at any time without prior notice.

No MALE can possibly know all The Rules;

If the FEMALE suspects the MALE knows all The Rules, she must immediately change some or all of The Rules.

The FEMALE is never wrong. If the FEMALE is wrong, it is due to a misunderstanding, which was the direct result of Something the MALE said or did which was wrong.

The MALE must apologise immediately for causing the said misunderstanding.

The MALE is always wrong.

The MALE may be right if he agrees with the FEMALE, unless she wants him to disagree.

The FEMALE may change her mind at any time.

The MALE may never change his mind without the express written consent of the FEMALE.

The FEMALE has every right to be angry or upset at any time.

The MALE must remain calm at all times, unless the

FEMALE wants him to be angry and /or upset.

The FEMALE, under no circumstances,will let the MALE know whether she wants him to be angry and/or upset.

The MALE is expected to mind-read at all times.
If the FEMALE has PMT, all The Rules are null and void.
The FEMALE is ready when she is ready.
The MALE must be ready at all times.

24 APPENDIX 08 GENDER FRENCH LANGUAGE

A French teacher was explaining to her class that in French, unlike English, nouns are designated as either masculine or feminine.

"House" is feminine-"la maison."

"Pencil" is masculine-"le crayon."

A student asked, "What gender is "computer'?"

Instead of giving the answer, the teacher split the class into two groups male and female - and asked them to decide for themselves whether "computer" should be a masculine or a feminine noun.

Each group was asked to give four reasons for their recommendation.

The Male Group

The men's group decided that "computer" should definitely be the feminine gender ("la Computer"), because:

1. No one but their creator understands their internal logic;

2. The native language they use to communicate with other computers is incomprehensible to everyone else;

3. Even the smallest mistakes are stored in long term memory for possible later review; and

4. As soon as you make a commitment to one, you find yourself spending half your salary on accessories for it.

The Female Group

The women's group, however, concluded that computers should be masculine gender ("le computer") because:

1. In order to do anything with them, you have to turn them on

2. They have a lot of data but still can't think for themselves;

3. They are supposed to help you solve problems, but half the time they are the problem; and as soon as you commit to one, you realize that if you could of waited a little longer, you could have got a better model!

The women won!!

25 Appendix 09: How Times Have Changed

Ladies can you please come back to reality. Remember you were made for your husband. An extract from Parish News Magazine.

TIPS TO LOOK AFTER YOUR HUSBAND

(Extract from 1950 Home Economics Book)

Have dinner ready: Plan ahead the night before to have a delicious meal on time. This is away of letting him know that you have been thinking about him and are concerned about his needs. Most men are hungry when they come home and the prospects of a good meal are part of the warm welcome needed.

Prepare Yourself: Take l 5 minutes to rest so you will be refreshed when he arrives. Touch up your make-up, put a ribbon in your hair and be fresh looking. He has just been with a lot of work weary people. Be a little gay and a little more interesting. His boring day may need a lift.

Clear away the clutter: Make one last trip through the main part of the house just before your husband arrives, gathering up school books, toys, paper, etc.. Then run a duster over the tables. Your husband will feel he has reached a haven of rest and order.

Prepare the Children: Take a few minutes to wash the children's hands and faces (if they are small), comb their hair and, if necessary, change their clothes. They are little treasures and he would like to see them playing the part.

Minimise all noise: At the time of his arrival eliminate all noise of washer, dryer, dishwasher or vacuum. Try to encourage the children to be quiet. Be happy to see him. Greet him with a warm smile.

Make him comfortable: Have him lean back in a comfortable chair or suggest he lie down in the bedroom. Have a cool or warm drink ready for him. Arrange his pillow and offer to take off his shoes. Speak in allow, soft, soothing voice. Allow him to relax and unwind.

Listen to him: You may have a dozen things to tell him but the moment of his arrival is not the time. Don't greet him with problems or complaints. Don't complain if he is late for dinner. Count this as minor compared with what he might have gone through that day. Let him talk first. Make the evening his. Never complain if he does not take you out to dinner or other places of entertainment. Try to understand his world of strain and pressure, his need to relax at home.

The goal: Make your home a place of peace and order where your husband can renew him self in body and spirit.

Authors Conclusion

The relationship between a man and women has always been a mystery to most men. And they will readily say that it is impossible to understand a women. It is my argument that if we ignore what God says to us, in scripture, about such relationships we are doomed to ignorance and will remain in the dark. Let scripture be our guide, believe every precept and obey its instruction, for this will be our wisdom.

OTHER PUBLICATIONS
These books are all available from our website
www.BiertonParticularBaptists.co.uk

Or view the books at:
Website:
A CASE OF CONSCIENCE RESOLVED

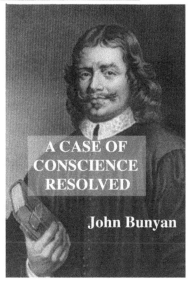

This exceedingly rare tract was first published in 1683, and was not reprinted, either separately, or in any edition of Bunyan's works.

At the time this case was drawn and submitted to Mr. Bunyan for his opinion, he was one of the most popular preachers in the kingdom, and universally esteemed in all the churches of Christ, for his profound knowledge of the sacred Scriptures. The question asked is:

Whether, where a Church of Christ is situate, it is the duty of the women of that congregation, ordinarily, and by appointment, to separate themselves from their brethren, and so to assemble together, to perform some parts of divine worship, as prayer, &c. without their men?

This was our question, this we debated, and this Mr. K. might have sent for, and have spoken to, since he will needs be a confuter. And, courteous reader, since I have here presented thee with the question

BEFORE THE COCK CROWS

BEFORE THE COCK
CROWS (PART 1)
Setting Captives Free
David Clarke

Part 1: The Daily Diary Of Trojan Horse International

David Clarke the Director of Trojan Horse International CM encountered remarkable opposition from various quarters in New Bilibid Prison, Muntinlupa City Philippines between October 2002 and July 2003. Most of those who opposed the mission were men from among Asia's most notorious criminals in the National Penitentiary, which is situated on the Reservation at Muntinlupa City, 1770, Philippines. If one were to judge the success of the mission by that amount of opposition that it experienced, then the mission was a remarkable success. Newton stated that to every force there is an equal but opposite one to oppose it and like Newton, David suggests that to every proactive work there is and equal but opposite reaction and so if this reaction were to be the measure of success, then the mission was remarkably successful. It also serves to demonstrate that God always triumphs. That God saves, not by might, but by His Spirit. That God puts to fight thousands of his enemies and empowers the one's and two's, that trust in Him in order to show that Salvation is truly of the Lord. This prison comprises of three Compounds and penal farms housing over 23,550 inmates, which are all under the control of the Department of Justice (DOJ) and the Bureau of Corrections. (BUCOR). The Chaplaincy, headed by Msgr. Helley Barrido, is responsible for all religious groups and voluntary work done within the Prison."Death Row" is in the Maximum Security Compound where over 1200 men are housed and they are all under the sentence of death. Some are doubly confirmed and due to be put to death by lethal injection. Trojan Horse International C.M. was established in the early part of 2001 and composed of a team of two from England, David Clarke and

Gordon John Smith. The mission was set up as a Christian ministry, seeking to bring assistance to Michael John Clarke, David's older brother, and many inmates at the Prison. This was where Michael had been incarcerated, for a crime he did not commit, and was serving a prison sentence of 16 years. He had been baptized as a Christian. In an old 45-gallon US Oil drum, on the 16th September 2000 in the Maximum Compound. Michael, like his brother David, had been converted from crime to Christ whilst suffering the bitter effects of this form of injustice in the Philippines. How ever Michaels conversion was some thirty years after David who had been brought up in Aylesbury, Buckinghamshire and had been converted from crime to Christ, at the age of 20 years old, on the 16th January 1970.

A BODY OF DOCTRINAL DIVINITY

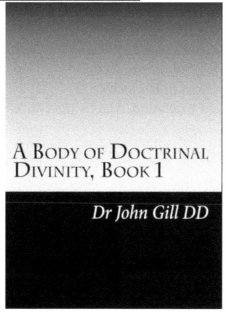

A System of Practical Truths
Authored by Dr John Gill DD, Created by David Clarke CertEd
List Price: $8.99
8.5" x 11" (21.59 x 27.94 cm)
Black & White on White paper
176 pages
ISBN-13: 978-1543085945
ISBN-10: 1543085946
THE FULL SET OF DR. JOHN GILL'S BODY OF DOCTRINAL DIVINITY IS IN SEVEN BOOKS. Available form our Office in the uk or Amazon.co.uk or Amazon.com

BOOK I
Of God, His Works, Names, Nature, Perfections And Persons.

BOOK II
Of The Acts And Works Of God

BOOK III
Of The External Works Of God

BOOk IV
Of The Acts Of The Grace Of God Towards And Upon His Elect In Time.

BOOK V
Of The Grace Of Christ In His States
Of Humiliation And Exaltation, And In The Offices Exercised By Jim In Them.

BOOK VI
Of The Blessings Of Grace, And The Doctrines Of It.

BOOK VII
Of The Final State Of Man

BIERTON STRICT AND PARTICULAR BAPTISTS
Including The Bierton Crisis

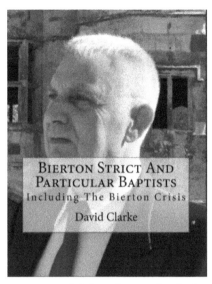

 This book tells the story and life of David Clarke in the form of an autobiography. It is no ordinary book in that David and his brother were both notorious criminals in the 60's, living in Aylesbury, Buckinghamshire, where they were MODs and were both sent to prison for and malicious wounding and carrying a fire arm without a license . They were however both converted from crime to Christ and turned their lives around. This story tells of David's conversion to Christianity in 1970 and that of Michael's conversion, 1999 some 30 years later. It tells of their time in HMP Canterbury Prison and David's time in HMP Wormwood Scrubs and Dover Borstal. It also tells of David's criminal activity and the crimes he committed before his miraculous conversion from crime to Christ, during a bad experience on LSD, in 1970. It tells how he became a Christian over night and how he learned to read in order to come to a fuller knowledge of the gospel. He learned to read through reading the bible and classical Christian literature. David tells of the events that led to him making a confession to the police about 24 crimes he had committed since leaving Dover Borstal in 1968 and of the court case where he was not sentenced. It tells how David's educated himself and went on to Higher education, and graduated with a Certificate in Education and how he went on to teach Electronics, for over 20 years, in colleges of Higher and Further Education. It tells of his life as a member of the Bierton Strict and Particular Baptist church, which was a Gospel Standard cause, and how he was called by the Lord and sent by the church to preach the gospel.

David tells of the various difficulties that he faced once he discovered the many doctrinal errors amongst the various Christian groups he met and of the opposition that he experience when he sought to correct them. David recorded his experience and finding in his book "The Bierton Crisis" 1984, written to help others. David's tells how his brother Michael was untouched by his conversion in 1970 and continued his flamboyant lifestyle ending up doing a 16 year prison sentence, in the Philippines, in 1996. David tells how Michael too was converted to Christianity through reading C.S. Lewis's book, "Mere Christianity", and him being convinced that Jesus was the Christ the Son of the living God. David then tells of his mission to the Philippines, to bring help and assistance to Michael, in 2001 and of their joint venture in helping in the rehabilitation of many former convicted criminals, not only in New Bilibid Prison but other Jails in the Philippines. David tells how he felt compelled to write this story in his book , "Converted On LSD Trip". once he got news of his brothers arrest, in the Philippines, via ITN Television news broadcast, in 1995. This book was published when he got news of his brothers conversion from crime to Christ in 1999, which was after serving 5 years of his 16 year sentence. This story is told in their joint book, "Trojan Warriors", that contains the testimonies of 66 notorious criminals who too had turned there lives around, from crime to Christ, 22 of which testimonies are men on Death Row. David say he believes his story could be of great help to any one seeking to follow the Lord Jesus Christ but sadly Michael died in New Bilibid Prison of tuberculosis, in 2005 before their vision of bringing help to many was realized.

Paperback: 356 pages
2 edition (16 Feb. 2015)
ISBN-10: 1519553285
ISBN-13: 978-1519553287
Product Dimensions: 13.3 x 2.1 x 20.3 cm
www.Amazon.co.uk

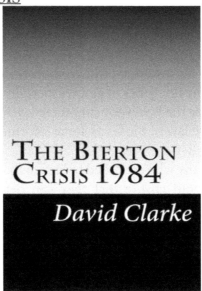

The Bierton Crisis is the personal story of David Clarke a member of the Bierton Strict and Particular Baptist church. He was also the church secretary and minister sent by the church to preach the gospel in 1982.

The Bierton Church was formed in 1832 and was a Gospel Standard cause who's rules of membership are such that only the church can terminate ones membership.

This tells of a crisis that took place in the church in 1984, which led to some members withdrawing support. David, the author, was one of the members who withdrew but the church did not terminate his membership as they wished him return.

This story tells in detail about those errors in doctrine and practices that had crept into the Bierton church and of the lengths taken to put matters right. David maintained and taught Particular Redemption and that the gospel was the rule of life for the believer and not the law of Moses as some church members maintained.

This story tells of the closure of the Bierton chapel when David was on mission work in the Philippines in December 2002 and when the remaining church members died. It tells how David was encouraged by the church overseer to return to Bierton and re-open the chapel.

On David's return to the UK he learned a newly unelected set of trustees had take over the responsibility for the chapel and were seeking to sell it. The story tells how he was refused permission to re open or use the chapel and they sold it as a domestic dwelling, in 2006.

102

These trustees held doctrinal views that opposed the Bierton church and they denied David's continued membership of the church in order to lay claim too and sell the chapel, using the money from the sale of the chapel for their own purposes.

David hopes that his testimony will promote the gospel of the Lord Jesus Christ, as set out in the doctrines of grace, especially Particular Redemption and the rule of life for the believer being the gospel of Christ, the royal law of liberty, and not the law of Moses as some reformed Calvinists teach, will be realized by the reader.

His desire is that any who are called to preach the gospel should examine their own standing and ensure that they can derive from scripture the doctrines and practices they teach and advance and that they can derived the truths they teach from scripture alone and not from the traditions of men or their opinions however well they may be thought of.

List Price: $11.99

5.25" x 8" (13.335 x 20.32 cm)

Black & White on White paper

256 pages

ISBN-13: 978-1508465959

ISBN-10: 1508465959

BISAC: Religion / Christian Theology / Apologetics

DIFFICULTIES ASSOCIATED WITH ARTICLES OF RELIGION

Among Particular Baptists

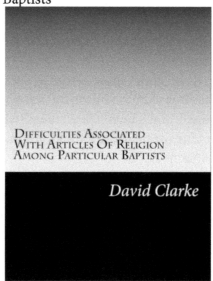

Articles of Religion are important when dealing with matters of the

Christian Religion, however problems occur when churches fail to recognize there is a growth in grace and knowledge of the Lord Jesus Christ in any believer. When a person first believes in the Lord Jesus Christ they cannot possibly have a comprehensive knowledge of a churches constitution or its articles of religion, before solemnly subscribing to them. The author David Clarke has introduced the Doctrines of Grace to Bierton Particular Baptists Pakistan, situated in Rahim Yar Khan, Pakistan and bearing in mind his own experience with articles of religion he has compiled Bierton Particular Baptists Pakistan articles of religion from the first Bierton Particular Baptists of 1831,of which he is the sole surviving member, the First London Baptist Confession, 2nd edition 1646, and those of Dr John Gill, in order to avoid some of the difficulties encounter by Particular Baptist during the later part of the 19 century and since. This booklet highlights the problem and suggests the Bierton Particular Baptists Pakistan is as step in the right direction.

Isaiah 52:8 Thy watchmen shall lift up the voice; with the voice together shall they sing: for they shall see eye to eye, when the LORD shall bring again Zion.

ISBN-13: 978-1532953446

BISAC: Religion / Christianity / Baptist

Contents

104

TROJAN WARRIORS

Setting Captives Free
Authored by Mr David Clarke CertEd, Authored by Mr Michael J Clarke
List Price: $15.99
5.25" x 8" (13.335 x 20.32 cm)
Black & White on White paper
446 pages
ISBN-13: 978-1508574989 (CreateSpace-Assigned)
ISBN-10: 1508574987
BISAC: Religion / Christian Life / General

Trojan Warriors is a true story of two brothers, Michael and David Clarke, who are brought up in Aylesbury, Buckinghamshire, England. They became criminals in the 60's and were sent to prison for malicious wounding and carrying a fire arm without a license, in 1967.

They both turned from their lives of crimes in remarkable ways but some

25 years apart, and then they worked together helping other prison inmates, on their own roads of reformation.

David the younger brother became a Christian, after a bad experience on LSD, in 1970, and then went on to educate himself and then on to Higher Education. He became a baptist minister and taught electronics for over 20 years, in colleges of Higher and Further Education. Michael however remained untouched and continued his flamboyant life style ending up serving a 16 year prison sentence, in the Philippines, in 1996, where he died of tuberculosis in 2005.

When David heard the news of his brothers arrest on an ITN television news bulletin he felt compelled to wrote their story. And then when he heard of his own brothers conversion from crime to Christ, after serving 5 year of his sentence, he published their story in his book, "Converted on LS Trip", and directed a mission of help to the Philippines to assist his brother. This book tells the story of this mission.

They then worked together with many former notorious criminals, who were inmates in New Bilibid Prison, who too had become Christians and turned their lives around. This help was to train them to become preachers of the gospel of Jesus Christ .

This book contains the 66 testimonies of some of these men who convicted former criminals, incarcerated in New Bilibid Prison. They are the, "Trojan Warriors", who had turned their lives around and from crime to Christ. Twenty two of these testimonies are men who are on Death Row scheduled to be executed by lethal injection.

Revelation 12 verse 11: And they overcame him by the blood of the lamb and the word of their testimony and they loved not their lives unto the death.

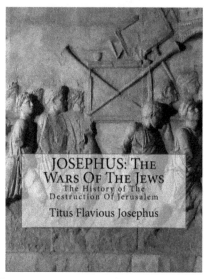

The History of The Destruction Of Jerusalem
Authored by Titus Flavius Josephus, Designed by Translated by William Winston

ISBN-13: 978-1985029132 (CreateSpace-Assigned)
ISBN-10: 1985029138
BISAC: Religion / Christianity / History / General
Josephus was an eye witness to those events that he records in this book, 'The Wars of The Jews', or 'The History of The Destruction Of Jerusalem'.

He records historic events that took place during and after the times of the New Testament scriptures.

The book of Revelation was a prophecy, given to Jesus Christ, and published by the Apostle John, about those things that were shortly to come to pass in his day.

From the internal evidence of the book Revelation was written before the Neuronic persecution, of 66 A.D. and before the fall off Jerusalem and the destruction of the temple, in 70. A.D. This is because the book records that the temple in Jerusalem was still standing at the time the book was written and not around 95 A.D. as Eusebius mistakenly says.

The historic events that Josephus records are remarkable as they give evidence to the fulfillment of Prophecy given by the Lord Jesus in his Olivet prophecy. In fact the book of Revelation was a prophecy of those events that were shortly to come to pass when Jesus spoke to John who wrote the

Revelation. Jesus had informed his Apostles about future events and they lived in expectation of there fulfillment in their day.

Josephus gives the historic evidence of the fulfillment of those prophecies and that confirms scripture fulfillment.

We recommend the James Stuart Russell's book, 'The Parousia' as a very good introduction to this subject and advertised at the back of this book in our Further Publications.

WHAT VERSION AUTHORIZED OR REVISED

Philp Mauro

The book discusses the issues relating to the reliably of the Authorised Version of the Bible and the failings of the so-called Revised Versions. It reminds the reader the greek printed text, produced by Erasmus in 1516, was derived from a broad set of 8 extant Greek manuscripts available to him in his day and in constant use by Christians to that day and not Latin bibles. Since1861 there has arisen those who claim the Authorised Version is not accurate and Wescott and Hort produced a new compiled Greek Printed text manuscript, derived from, and base upon, two 4th C handwritten extant manuscripts. Codex Sinaiticus, written in Greek and Codec's Vaticanus, written in Latin. They claimed that since these manuscripts were the oldest extant manuscripts in the world (400 years after the original writing of the new testament scriptures) they were far superior and more reliable than the text underlying the Authorised version of the bible.And since 1945 all Bible translations are based upon the New Greek manuscript text of Wescott and Hort published in 1861. This is an eclectic text and not the Received Text

108

used by the translator of the Authorised Version of the Bible and know by
Christians, throughout the Christian age, as the Word of God.It has been
republished by Bierton Particular Baptist to educate serious minded people
about the subject of Bible translations and support the Authorised version
of the Bible.Philip Mauro was a lawyer in America, who practiced before
the Supreme Court.He prepared briefs NOTES for the Scopes Trial WHICH
was an American legal case in July 1925 THAT had made it unlawful to
teach human evolution in any state-funded school.[1] The trial publicized
the Fundamentalist-Modernist controversy, which set Modernists, who said
evolution was not inconsistent with religion,[4] against Fundamentalists,
who said the word of God as revealed in the Bible took priority over all
human knowledge. The case was thus seen as both a theological contest and
a trial on whether "modern science" should be taught in schools. Mauro was
ALSO passenger on the British ocean liner RMS Carpathia when it rescued
the passengers of the Titanic in April 1912.It is hoped that this book will
rescue any that are sinking in the sea of the natural Modern man's opinion
as to the reliability of the Authorised Version the bible.

A COMMENTARY ON THE GOSPEL OF MATTHEW

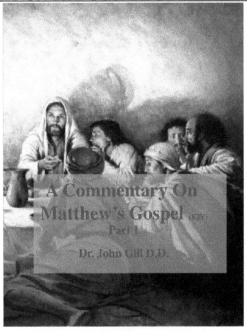

By John Gill

The Gospel According to Matthew was the first written gospel and
published sometime between (AD 31-38). It was written before Mark's (AD
38-44) and Luke's Gospel (AD-61).

109

Matthew was a Jew and one of the 12 Apostles of the Lord Jesus Christ and named Levi. He was a tax collector for the Romans. There are two strong traditions that Matthew made a personal copy of his gospel and gave it to Barnabas, a companion of the Apostle Paul.

Matthew tells of the birth and lineage of Jesus. The life death, resurrection of the Lord Jesus Christ and the final words of Jesus before his ascension into heaven.

This publication is presented knowing that Matthew penned his gospel that contains all those things the Lord Jesus wanted him to publish.

Matthew records the Olivet prophesy of Jesus concerning those fearful things that were to come to pass within the period of that generation and after his ascension.

It is the intention of the publisher that this will assist in making the gospel known to all people and is published in two parts PART 1 chapter 1 to 16. And PART 2 chapter 17 to 28.

WHAT HAPPENED IN A.D. 70

Ed. Stevens

This book introduces a view of Bible prophecy which many have found extremely helpful in their Bible study. It explains the end time riddles which have always bothered students of Bible prophecy. It is a consistent view which makes the book of Revelation much easier to understand. It establishes when the New Testament canon of scripture was completed, demolishes the liberal attack on the inspiration of the New Testament, and is more conservative on most other issues than traditional views. And there is no compromise of any essential Biblical doctrine of the Christian faith.

The key to understand any passage of scripture has always been a good grasp of the historical setting in which it was originally written {audience relevance). Two thousand yeas from now our history, culture, politics and language will have changed dramatically. Imagine someone then having to learn the ancient language of "American English" to read our USA newspapers! If they saw one of our political cartoons with a donkey and elephant, what would they think? How would they go about understanding it? Not only would they have to study the language, but also our culture, history, politics and economics. The same applies to Bible study. If we are really going to understand what all the "donkeys and elephants" (beasts, harlots, dragons, etc.) Symbolize in the book of Revelation, we will have to seriously and carefully study the language, history, culture and politics of the First Century. Of course, the truths essential for salvation are couched in simple language that everyone can grasp. But there are numerous scriptures in the Bible which are "hard to understand" (cf. 2 Pet 3:16), and Bible prophecy is one of those things which must be approached with much more focus on the original historical art cultural context (audience relevance)

One of the main purposes of this book is to provide a closer look at the historical framework behind the New Testament. Many hove found it helpful to lay aside (at least temporarily) the legion of speculative opinions about the book of Revelation, and look at a more historical alternative, which is that the book of Revelation was written to the first century church and had primary relevance to them. It warned of events that were about to happen in their lifetime, and prepared them for the tribulation and other events associated with the End of the Jewish Age.

Atheists, skeptics, Jew, Muslims, and liberal critics of the bible use the supposed failure of those end times events to occur in the First Century to undermine the integrity of Christs and the inspired NT writings.

Non-Christian Jews laugh at this supposed non-occurrence, and use it as evidence that Jesus is not the Messiah. Their forefathers in the flesh rejected Jesus in His first coming because He did not fulfill the Old Testament prophecies in the materialistic and nationalistic way that they were expecting, even though Jesus told them that His Kingdom was not of this world, and that it would be within them instead. Yet it seems that many futurists today are expecting that same kind of materialistic and nationalistic kingdom to arrive at a future return of Christ Are they making the same mistake about the Second Coming that the Jews made about His first coming? Jesus repeatedly said His Kingdom is "not of this world" and that it would "not come with observation." It is a spiritual entity, and it has arrived We live in it. Both futurist Christians and non-Christian Jews need to realize this.

Christians are finally beginning to seek alternatives to the fatally flawed futurist interpretation. This book introduces the Preterist view.

"Preterist" simply means past in fulfillment It means that Christ has already fulfilled His promise to return and consummate redemption in Himself and His ongoing spiritual kingdom (the church). We should be like the noble-minded Bereans and "search the scriptures daily to see whether these things are true" You might want to have your Bible open alongside as you read.

Edward E. Stevens
INTERNATIONAL PRETERIST ASSOCIATION
*h*ttps://www.preterist.org/
Bradford, Pennsylvania
April 17,2010

THE FINAL DECADE BEFORE THE END

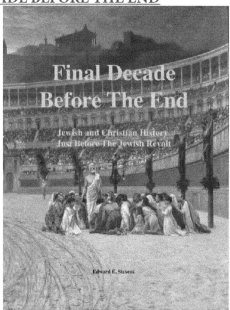

Ed. Stevens

Ever since the booklet, **What Happened In AD 70?** was published in 1980, there have been constant requests for more detailed information about the Destruction of Jerusalem and the Jewish, Roman, and Christian history associated with it. Over the years since then I have studied Josephus,

Yosippon, Hegesippus, Tacitus, Suetonius, Eusebius, the Talmud, Midrash, Zohar, Pseudepigrapha, Church Fathers, Apocrypha, Dead Sea Scrolls and other Jewish/Christian writings, trying to determine exactly what happened, when it happened, and the effect it had upon the Church.

Then in 2002, after I began to promote J. S. Russell's view of a literal rapture, the demand for historical documentation of the fulfillment of all eschatological events dramatically increased. That forced me to dig much deeper. So in 2007 I put together a 21-page chronology of first century events. Two years later in 2009, we published a more substantial 73-page manuscript entitled, First Century Events in Chronological Order. That helped fill the void, but it did not go far enough. It only increased the appetite for a more detailed and documented historical reconstruction of first century events.

The book of Acts does not give a lot of details about the other Roman and Jewish events that were happening while Paul was on his various missionary journeys. For those events, we have to go to the other contemporary Jewish and Roman historians such as Josephus and Tacitus. The closer we get to AD 70, the more important all of those Jewish and Roman events become. They form an important backdrop behind the Christian events, and show how all the predictions made by Jesus were literally fulfilled. Every High Priest and Zealot leader that we encounter from AD 52 onwards are directly connected with the events of the Last Days. Things are heating up, not only for the Christians, but also for the Jews and the Romans.

Paul on his missionary journeys was clearly following a plan which was providentially arranged for him by Christ: (1) to plant new churches among all nations and not just Jews, (2) appoint elders and deacons in every church (Acts 14:23; 1 Cor. 4:17), (3) write inspired epistles to guide them, (4) instruct his fellow workers to "teach these things to faithful men who would be able to teach others also" (2 Tim. 2:2), and (5) establish the Gentiles in the Church and make them one united body with the Jews (Eph 4). Everywhere Paul went, he followed this pattern. We see this clearly as we study the historical narrative in Acts and Paul's other epistles that were written during this time. These are essential patterns that the apostles evidently bound upon both Gentile and Jewish Christians, and which were intended to be the pattern for all future generations of the eternal Church (Eph 3:21; 2Tim 2:2).

We begin our study by looking at the most likely dates for Matthew (AD 31-38) and Mark (AD 38- 44), and then proceed to the first three epistles of Paul (Galatians, 1 & 2 Thessalonians), which were written on his second missionary journey (AD 51-53). Including these five books in our study allows us to date all twenty-seven books of our New Testament, and show

113

how the NT canon was formed and completed before the outbreak of the Jewish War in AD 66. The study of New Testament canonization in itself is a good reason for reading this work, without even looking at the historical fulfillment of all of the endtime prophecies that we document here.

After looking at the dates for those first five books, we then move on into the third missionary journey of Apostle Paul which began in AD 54. It was during this final dozen years (from AD 54 until AD 66) when the birth pangs and signs of the end started increasing in both intensity and frequency, along with a quickening pace of NT books being written. We show how 19 of our 27 NT books (70 percent) were written during those last five years just before the Neronic persecution (AD 60-64). The Great Commission was finished, and the rest of the endtime events predicted in the Olivet Discourse were fulfilled during that time of "tribulation" upon the church and the "days of vengeance" upon the unbelieving Jews (Luke 21:22).

Edward E. Stevens
INTERNATIONAL PRETERIST ASSOCIATION
https://www.preterist.org
Bradford, Pennsylvania
April 17,2010

THE PAROUSIA 2ND EDITION

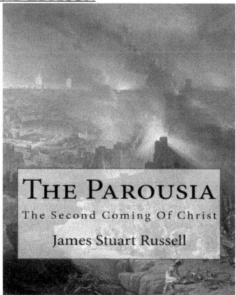

The Second Coming Of Christ
Authored by James Stuart Russell, Preface by Mr David Clarke, Preface by Dr Don K Preston DD

A reformation – indeed – a revolution of sorts is taking place in modern evangelical Christianity. And while many who are joining in and helping promote this movement are not even aware of it, the book you hold in your hand has contributed greatly to initiating this new reformation. This "new" movement is sometimes called full preterism, (Also, and preferably by this writer, Covenant Eschatology). It is the belief that all Bible prophecy is fulfilled.

The famous evangelist Charles H. Spurgeon was deeply impressed with the scholarly, solid research in the book, although he did not accept the "final" conclusions reached by Russell. In modern times, this work has, and continues to impress those who read it. The reason is simple, the New Testament is emphatic and unambiguous in positing Christ's coming and the end of the age for the first century generation. To say this has troubled both scholars and laymen alike is an understatement of massive proportions.

This book first appeared in 1878 (anonymously), and again in 1887 with author attribution. The book was well known in scholarly circles primarily and attracted a good bit of attention, both positive and negative. The public, however, seemed almost unaware of the stunning conclusions and the research supporting those conclusions, until or unless they read of Russell's work in the footnotes of the commentaries.

Scholars have recognized and grappled with this imminence element, that is the stated nearness of the day of the Lord, seldom finding satisfactory answers. Scholars such as David Strauss accused Jesus of failure. Later, Bultmann said that every school boy knows that Jesus predicted his coming and the end of the world for his generation, and every school boy knows it did not happen. C.S. Lewis also could not resolve the apparent failed eschatology. Bertrand Russell rejected Christianity due to the failed eschatology - as he perceived it - of Jesus and the Bible writers. As a result of these "skeptical" authors, modern Bible scholarship has followed in their path and Bible commentaries today almost casually assert the failure of the Bible writers - and Jesus - in their eschatological predictions.

This is where Russell's work is of such importance. While Russell was not totally consistent with his own arguments and conclusions, nonetheless, his work is of tremendous importance and laid the groundwork for the modern revolution known as the preterist movement.

Russell systematically addressed virtually every New Testament prediction of the eschaton. With incisive clarity and logical acumen, he sweeps aside the almost trite objections to the objective nature of the Biblical language of imminence. With excellent linguistic analysis, solid hermeneutic and powerful exegetical skills, Russell shows that there is no way to deny that Jesus and his followers not only believed in a first century, end of the age parousia, but, they taught it as divine truth claiming the inspiration of the Holy Spirit as their authority.

Russell not only fully established the undeniable reality of the first century imminence of "the end," he powerfully and carefully shares with the reader that "the end" that Jesus and the N.T. writers were anticipating was not the end of the time space continuum (end of the world). It was in fact, the end of the Old Covenant Age of Israel that arrived with the cataclysmic destruction of Jerusalem and the Temple in AD 70. Russell properly shows how the traditional church has so badly missed the incredible significance of the end of that Old Covenant Age.

Russell's work is a stunning rejection – and corrective -- of what the "Orthodox" historical "Creedal" church has and continues to affirm. The reader may well find themselves wondering how the "divines" missed it so badly! Further, the reader will discover that Russell's main arguments are an effective, valid and true assessment of Biblical eschatology. And make no mistake, eschatology matters.

THE TOTAL DEPRAVITY OF MAN

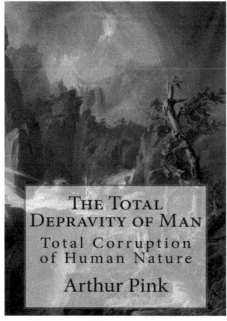

THE TOTAL
DEPRAVITY OF MAN
Total Corruption
of Human Nature

Arthur Pink

This republication of A.W. Pink's work,

The Total Depravity of Man, is intended to introduce Christians, of this generation, to those truths that seem to have been lost among Evangelical Christians. It is believed that a right understanding of man's fall in Adam will lead the believer to see the necessity salvation by the a sovereign choice, by God, of men to salvation and the reality of particular redemption. These doctrines are known as the doctrines of grace some times referred to as Calvinism. These truth are held by Particular Baptists to this day as can be read in the First London Baptist Confession of faith, of 1644. These truths have met with opposition from various quarters resulting in controversy not only from Arminian's but also among Calvinists. It is intended that his book will help the believer come to a biblical understanding of the total depravity and inability for man to save him self and that mans salvation depended entirely upon the grace and mercy of God alone. That the gospel of Christ declares this truth very clearly and is the antidote to all false religion.

LET CHRISTIAN MEN BE MEN

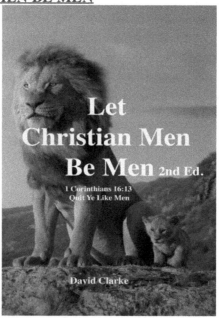

ASIN : B09QFDVDR8
Publisher : Independently published (15 Jan. 2022)
Language : English
Paperback : 287 pages
ISBN-13 : 979-8402754034
Dimensions : 15.24 x 1.65 x 22.86 cm

This was originally published as The Bierton Crisis 1984 and is the personal story of David Clarke a member of the Bierton Strict and Particular Baptist church. He was also the church secretary and minister sent by the church to preach the gospel in 1982.

The Bierton Church was formed in 1832 and was a Gospel Standard cause who's rules of membership are such that only the church can terminate ones membership.

This tells of a crisis that took place in the church in 1984, which led to some members withdrawing support. David, the author, was one of the members who withdrew but the church did not terminate his membership as they wished him return.

This story tells in detail about those errors in doctrine and practices that had crept into the Bierton church and of the lengths taken to put matters right. David maintained and taught Particular Redemption and that the gospel was the rule of life for the believer and not the law of Moses as some church members maintained.

This story tells of the closure of the Bierton chapel when David was on mission work in the Philippines in December 2002 and when the remaining church members died. It tells how David was encouraged by the church overseer to return to Bierton and re-open the chapel.

On David's return to the UK he learned a newly unelected set of trustees had take over the responsibility for the chapel and were seeking to sell it. The story tells how he was refused permission to re open or use the chapel and they sold it as a domestic dwelling, in 2006.

These trustees held doctrinal views that opposed the Bierton church and they denied David's continued membership of the church in order to lay claim too and sell the chapel, using the money from the sale of the chapel for their own purposes.

David hopes that his testimony will promote the gospel of the Lord Jesus Christ, as set out in the doctrines of grace, especially Particular Redemption and the rule of life for the believer being the gospel of Christ, the royal law of liberty, and not the law of Moses as some reformed Calvinists teach, will be realized by the reader.

His desire is that any who are called to preach the gospel should examine their own standing and ensure that they can derive from scripture the doctrines and practices they teach and advance and that they can derived the truths they teach from scripture alone and not from the traditions of men or their opinions however well they may be thought of.

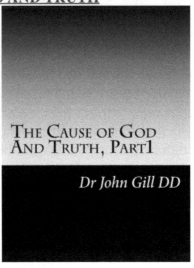

Authored by Dr John Gill DD,
Created by Rev David Clarke Cert E
ISBN-13: 978-1530739912
ISBN-10: 1530739918
THERE ARE FOUR BOOKS

Book 1 is Part 1

Deals with the scriptures sighted by Dr Whiby in   support of a universal scheme of salvation.

Book 2 is Part 2

Treats the subject Reprobation, Redemption Efficacious grace, Corruption of human nature and Perseverance. .

Book 3 is Part 3

Treats the Doctrines of grace, Reprobation, election and reprobation, Redemption, efficacious grace freedom of the will perseverance of the saints the providence of God the state and case of the heathen.

Book 4 is Part 4

And treats The Doctrines of Grace and the church fathers.

The following works were undertaken and begun about the year 1733 or 1734, at which time Dr. Whitby's Discourse on the Five Points was reprinting, judged to be a masterpiece on the subject, in the English tongue, and accounted an unanswerable one ; and it was almost in the mouth of every one, as an **objection to the Calvinists.**

Why do not ye answer Dr. Whitby ? Induced hereby, I determined to give it another reading, and found myself inclined to answer it, and thought this was a very proper and seasonable time to engage in such a work.

In the year 1735, the First Part of this work was published, in which are considered the several passages of Scripture made use of by Dr. Whitby and others in favour of the Universal Scheme, and against the Calvinistic Scheme, in which their arguments and objections are answered, and the several passages set in a just and proper light. These, and what are contained in the following part in favour of the particular scheme, are extracted from sermons delivered in a Wednesday evening's lecture.

The second part was published in the year 1736, in which the several passages of Scripture in favour of special and distinguishing grace, and the arguments from them, are vindicated from the exceptions of the Arminian, and particularly from Dr. Whitby, and a reply made to answers and objections to them.

BORSTAL BOYS

Alternatively From Crime To Christ

Authored by Mr David Clarke Cert. Ed.

"Borstal Boys" is a special edition of the author's original title, "Converted on LSD" and written for prison inmates.

It tells the story of two brothers, Michael and David Clarke, who grew up in Aylesbury, in the 60's. They were Mods but Michael spent two spells in Oxford Detention Center, referred to as the short sharp shock treatment, and then Rochester Borstal, during which time David inherited his brothers Lambretta scooter a T.V. 175, in 1966. It was then he lived in the light and fame of his brothers notoriety with the Aylesbury Mods.

On Michael's release from Borstal in 1966 these brothers teamed up together and were soon sent to prison for malicious wounding and carrying a fire arm without a license. Michael was sent to Maidstone Prison and David to Dover Borstal.

On leaving Dover Borstal in 1968, Dave had a three year career of undetected crime until he was arrested but not by the police. He had a bad experience on LSD, on the 16th January, 1970 and called out to God for help. As a result

he became Christian and turned from crime overnight and went on the straight and narrow.

The story tells how David learned to read and educate himself, went on to Higher Education and became a Baptist minister and a Lecturer teaching electronics of over 20 years in colleges of higher and Further Education. His brother Michael however was unaffected and continued his flamboyant and criminal life style and ended up in prison in the Philippines 25 years later, serving a 16 year sentence.

The book tells how David was prompted to write his story in his book, "Converted on LSD Trip" when he got news of his brothers arrest and imprisonment in the Philippines, in 1995. It tells of his brothers conversion from crime to Christ, in 1999 and the work they did jointly to bring help to others.

It tells how these Borstal Boys, Michael and David Clarke, worked to asset and help many convicted criminals on their road to reformation. This part of the story is told in their joint book, "Trojan Warriors" that contains 66 testimonies of notorious convicted criminals in New Bilibid Prison, who had turned their lives around from crime to Christ, 22 of which were on Death Row scheduled to be executed by lethal injection.

Borstal Boys is a special edition written for prison inmates, 250 copies of which have been sent, at the request of prison chaplains, to 20 prisons in the UK and tells the good and the bad happenings of two brothers who turned the lives around and from crime to Christ.

The story is currently being written as a Punk Rock opera called "Borstal Boy", scheduled to be performed in prisons.

THE WEST AND THE QURAN

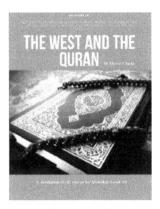

A Translation of The Quran

By David Clarke

This Publication treats the subject of the Quran and the reason for presenting this is due to a rise in Islamic terrorism which has caused great concern to many in the West. So with the current massive influx of Muslim's migrating from the various parts of the world into Europe, Great Britain and the USA, it seems reasonable to discover the roots of Islam in order to deal with the problems that have occurred. Our Politicians seem clueless on how to deal with this enemy and when they are questioned they appear to know relatively little about Muhammad and his teaching. One of our greatest Prime-ministers in Britain William Gladstone declared the Quran an "Accursed book" and once held a copy of Muhammad's Quran up in Parliament, declaring: "So long as there is this book there will be no peace in the world". Winston Churchill was one of the greatest leaders of the 20th Century, who served as Prime Minister of the United Kingdom during World War II and again from 1951 to 1955. As an officer of the British Army in 1897 and 1898, he fought against a Pashtun tribe in the north west frontier of British India and also at the Battle of Omdurman in Sudan. In both of those conflicts, he had eye-opening encounters with Muslims. These incidents allowed his keen powers of observation and always-fluid pen to weigh in on the subject of Islamic society. While these words were written when he was only 25-years-old (in 1899), they serve as a prophetic warning to Western civilisation today. "How dreadful are the curses which Mohammedanism (Islam) lays on its votaries! Besides the fanatical frenzy, which is as dangerous in a man as hydrophobia in a dog, there is this fearful fatalistic apathy." Churchill apparently witnessed the same phenomenon in several places he visited. "The effects are apparent in many countries: improvident habits, slovenly systems of agriculture, sluggish methods of commerce and insecurity of property exist wherever the followers of the Prophet rule or live." He saw the temporal and the eternal tainted by their belief system. "A degraded sensualism deprives this life of its grace and refinement, the next of its dignity and sanctity," he wrote. The second-class status of women also grated at the young officer. "The fact that in Mohammedan law every woman must belong to some man as his absolute property, either as a child, a wife, or a concubine, must delay the final extinction of slavery until the faith of Islam has ceased to be a great power among men," he noted. "Individual Muslims may show splendid qualities, but the influence of the religion paralyses the social development of those who follow it. No stronger retrograde force exists in the world." Well before the birth of modern Israel, its terror tactics and drive for world domination were felt. "Far from being moribund, Mohammedanism is a militant and proselytising faith. It has already spread throughout Central Africa, raising fearless warriors at every step, and were it not that Christianity is sheltered in the strong arms of science, the science against which it (Islam) has vainly struggled, the civilisation of modern Europe might fall, as fell the civilisation of ancient Rome." With the influx of Muslim people from the various parts of the continent along with their culture all of which is shaped by the teachings of Muhammad in the Quran. Some objections and Observations are as follows: Islam means submission Islam does not mean peace Multiculturalism is a failure. Islam denies the natural rights of women An Objection Halal Meat An Objection To Shari-ah Law Objects to Female Genital Mutilation (FGM) An objection to Jihad which seeks over throw Western culture through education, Social activity, political activation and Law. For this reason, this publication is made available for education purposes. With this prayer that God may grant us all wisdom as to how we may respond to the rise and threat of Islam.

CHRIST ALONE EXALTED

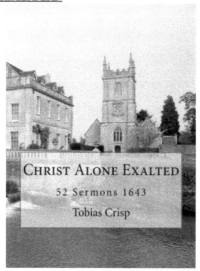

In 3 volumes

Tobias Crisp was preacher of the gospel in England. He was born in 1600 and died in 1643 at which time these 13 sermons were first published. Within 3 years further sermons were published in further volumes this is the first. He lived at the time when The First London Baptist Confession of Faith 1644 was being prepared for publishing and it is clear from these sermons he taught Calvinistic truths. He preached the doctrines of grace and was charged with being an Antinomian and provoked opposition from various quarters. Dr John Gill in defence of Crisp republished these sermons along with his own notes showing that Tobias Crisps taught clearly the truths of the lord Jesus Christ

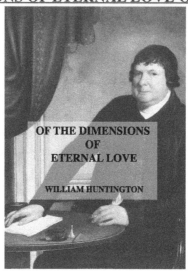

by William Huntington (Author), David Clarke (Editor)
William Huntington treats the subject of the eternal, and everlasting love of God which is displayed in the salvation of the elect. He demonstrates that the elect were chosen by the Father, redeemed by the Son and set apart by the Spirit, when called to believe. He shows that this love is peculiar to the elect and not upon all of Adam's fallen world.

SPEAKING ENGAGEMENTS
David Clarke is available for speaking Engagements in the UK and abroad.